The **AA** 100 Best W...
Scotland

Produced by AA Publishing
© Automobile Association Developments
Limited 2004
Reprinted 2005

Published by AA Publishing (a trading name
of Automobile Association Developments
Limited, whose registered office is
Southwood East, Apollo Rise, Farnborough,
Hampshire, GU14 0JW; registered number
1878835)

Ordnance Survey® This product includes
mapping data licensed
from Ordnance Survey® with the permission
of the Controller of Her Majesty's Stationery
Office.
© Crown copyright 2005. All rights reserved.
Licence number 399221

ISBN-10: 0 7495 4051 6
ISBN-13: 978 0 7495 4051 6
A02604

A CIP catalogue record for this book is
available from the British Library.

Please write to:
AA Publishing, FH16, Fanum House,
Basing View, Basingstoke RG21 4EA

These routes appear in the *AA Local Walks*
series and *1001 Walks in Britain*.

Visit AA Publishing at:
www.theAA.com/bookshop

Colour reproduction by:
Keene Group, Andover
Printed and bound by:
Oriental Press, Dubai

Acknowledgements

Written and researched by Kate Barrett,
Rebecca Ford, Ronald Turnbull, Hugh Taylor
and Moira McCrossan

Picture credits

All images are held in the Automobile
Association's own photo library (AA World
Travel Library) and were taken by the
following photographers:
Front cover S Day; 3 S Gibson; 4/5 R Weir;
6/7 A J Hopkins; 8/9 P Sharpe;
11tl S Anderson; 11tr S Day;
11cr S Anderson; 12tl K Paterson;
12tr S Day; 12cl M Alexander; 13 R Weir.

*Opposite: The Falls of Clyde,
New Lanark
Page 4: The impressive ruins of
12th-century St Andrews
Cathedral*

Contents

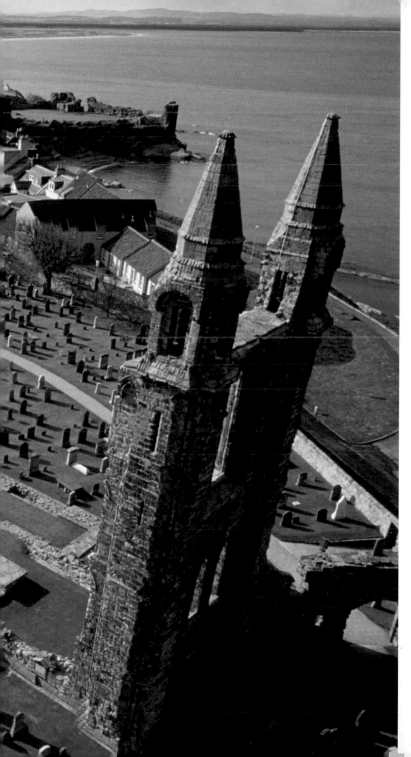

Beinn Edra and Trotternish
Ridge from the Quiraing on the
Isle of Skye

Scotland

Almost half the size of England, yet with barely one fifth of its population, Scotland is a country of huge spaces and mountains on a grand scale. It is also a nation steeped in history and cultural diversity.

A winding road runs through the majestic mountain pass of Glen Coe

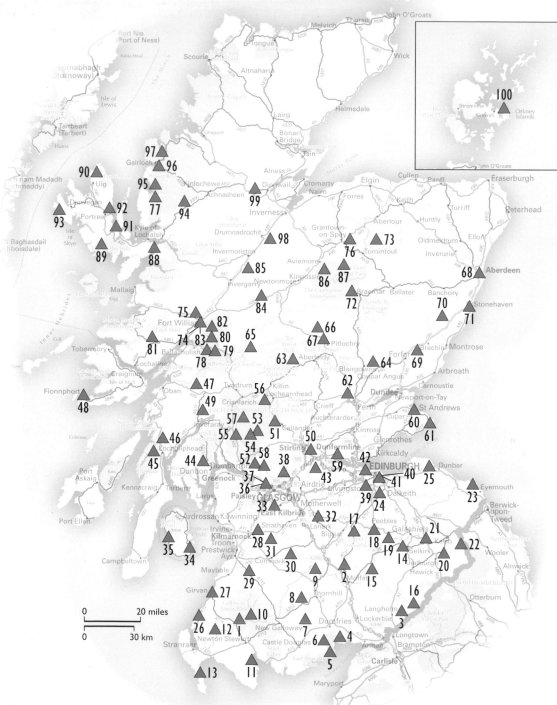

Scotland

Vast fjord-like lochs penetrating to the heart of the highest mountains – this is how we perceive the Scottish identity, and yet it is only part of the story. In the east the border lands with their rounded hilltops and deep valleys produce tales and people very different from the Celtic 'kilts' of the west. The southwest also has Celtic origins mixed up with ancient Britons, and with Irish and Viking traditions.

The Southern Uplands form a barrier between the Scots and the English, and in doing so host some of the most colourful and bloody chapters in Scotland's history. To the east, the high, rounded Borders have harboured proud families. In late medieval times they were the reivers, striking into England to take cattle and pillage their impoverished neighbours. The Union of the Crowns ended this lawlessness, but their balladry lived on and was immortalised by Robert Burns, Sir Walter Scott, and later by Hugh MacDiarmid.

In the southwest religious conflict in the 17th century tore families apart and culminated in the 'killing times', when troops loyal to the Crown were set against Presbyterian worshippers and many hundreds died.

The central belt is where Scotland's Industrial Revolution set the country on course to

become the engine of the British Empire. From the Clydeside yards came the ships that kept a maritime kingdom playing on a world stage. The rival cities of Edinburgh and Glasgow vie for supremacy. Glasgow has the people, the football teams and the architecture of Charles Rennie Macintosh; Edinburgh has the political and royal capitals, the festival and the tourists.

But it is the Highlands that have come to define Scotland. Barely have you left Glasgow's northern suburbs and their breathtaking panoramas come into view. It is no coincidence that Loch Lomond is at the heart of Scotland's first National Park. There are many differences in the Highland scene as you travel from west to east. The western mountains are jagged and rise up fiercely from the glens. In the east

Left: Scenic Glen Trool
Above: The shores of Loch Lomond
Right: Ruined Jedburgh Abbey

they are less spiky, but no less massive. On both sides of the A9 you'll find deep valleys and lochs. The clear waters of the Spey Valley have long been famous for salmon fishing and as an ingredient in whisky.

The Southern Uplands
The size of the Southern Uplands always comes as a surprise. The scale of the Devil's Beeftub, near Moffat, will cause you to catch your breath. You will understand why the Tweed Valley commands so great a place in history when you follow this great river as it winds away from Peebles or Dryburgh. Other border towns have their own stories. Selkirk was the birthplace of the explorer

Mungo Park. Mary, Queen of Scots came close to death from a fever while staying in a house near Jedburgh Abbey and at Traquair you'll find the oldest inhabited residence in Scotland. The Uplands continue into the southwest. The Nith Estuary and the Solway are guarded by the astonishing three-cornered stronghold of Caerlaverock Castle. Further west, Wigtown's

notoriety stems from the execution by drowning of two Covenanter women in 1685.

Industrial Origins
Looking back up the Nith Valley and its tributaries, the pretty village of Moniaive has long been attractive to artists and, in nearby Glenkiln, you'll find a whole valley dedicated to sculpture. The immense iron foundries at

Left: The harbour at St Abbs
Above: Edinburgh Castle
Right: Ben Nevis

Andrews. Visit the amazing Falkirk Wheel, joining the Forth and Clyde Canal with the Union Canal, and making east–west navigation possible again. And if you are in the mood for canal walking the Kilsyth tow path on the Forth and Clyde can be combined with a return along the Antonine Wall.

Highland Vision

From the Byne Hill in Ayrshire, Ailsa Craig stands prominently in the Firth of Clyde. Here you can glimpse the Highlands as the peaks of Arran rise from the sea. Another ferry will take you to the Cowal Peninsula, where Puck's Glen is a lovely corner of the former Benmore Estate with an internationally important botanic garden. Glasgow folk flocked to

such semi-wild sites and found resorts and refuges at places such as Carbeth, Aberfoyle and Loch Katrine.

The Highlands offer some of the best walking in Britain – to the Hidden Valley of Glen Coe, beneath the slopes of Ben Nevis and on Skye where the weirdly shaped Quiraing is fascinating to explore. Little Raasay will give an island experience all by itself, and Portree makes a fine base for a gentle walk with fine views.

Mull, too, is worth crossing to, even if just to hop over to Iona, where Scottish kings were laid to rest. It rivals Kilmartin Glen in importance in Scottish history, but cannot claim the crowning stones of Dunadd.

Dunaskin were created because of the abundance of raw materials in the area, and today you can visit the visitor centre and walk among the ruins of the deserted workers' village. The industrial site of New Lanark, where Robert Owen's planned mill town is now a World Heritage Site.

Heart of the Nation

Several places claim to be the heart of Scotland, but Edinburgh is among the most worthy. This city commands several walks – up to its castle and around its Georgian New Town. Edinburgh's backcloth is formed by the Pentland Hills, an odd corner of mountain rising from an upland plateau. Hidden on its northern flank is mysterious Rosslyn Glen, with its chapel and castle. Before you are done with the south, visit St Abb's Head, then head across the Forth to Culross and St

To the East

This is the home of the Scots pine and woodlands. You'll find royal stories and whisky to pursue at Braemar and Glenlivet. At the mouth of Glen Tilt stands Blair Athol, where the Duke raised his own army, while Glen Prosen opens out to Kirriemuir, the birthplace of J M Barrie. And Stirling spans the gap between Highland and Lowland.

Using this Book

❶ Information panels
Information panels show the total distance and total amount of ascent (that is how much ascent you will accumulate throughout the walk). An indication of the gradient you will encounter is shown by the rating 0–3. Zero indicates fairly flat ground and 3 indicates undulating terrain with several very steep slopes.

❷ Minimum time
The minimum time suggested is for approximate guidance only. It assumes reasonably fit walkers and doesn't allow for stops.

❸ Start points
The start of each walk is given as a six-figure grid reference prefixed by two letters indicating which 100km square of the National Grid it refers to.

You'll find more information on grid references on most Ordnance Survey maps.

❹ Abbreviations
Walk directions use these abbreviations:
L – left
L–H – left-hand
R – right
R–H – right-hand
Names which appear on signposts are given in brackets, for example ('Bantam Beach').

❺ Suggested maps
Details of appropriate maps are given for each walk, and usually refer to 1:25,000 scale Ordnance Survey Explorer maps. We strongly recommend that you always take the appropriate OS map with you. Our hand-drawn maps are there to give you the route and do not

Braemar Castle on Royal Deeside dates from 1628

show all the details or relief that you will need to navigate around the routes provided in this collection. You can purchase OS maps at all good bookshops, or by calling Stanfords on 020 7836 2260.

❻ Car parking
Many of the car parks suggested are public, but occasionally you may find you

have to park on the roadside or in a lay-by. Please be considerate when you leave your car, ensuring that access roads or gates are not blocked and that other vehicles can pass safely. Remember that pub car parks are private and should not be used unless you are visiting the pub or you have the landlord's permission to park there.

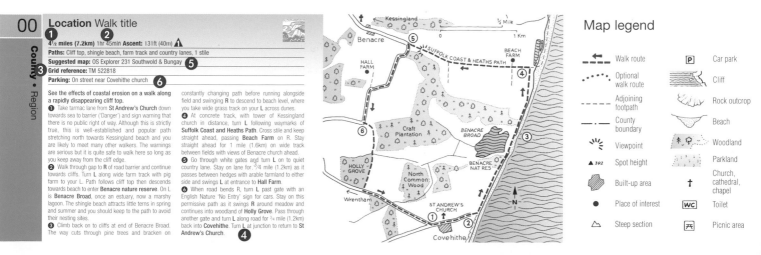

1 Glentrool The Battle of Independence

5 miles (8km) 2hrs **Ascent:** 151ft (46m)
Paths: Forest trails, metalled roads, 1 stile
Suggested map: OS Explorer 318 Galloway Forest Park North
Grid reference: NX 396791
Parking: Entrance to Caldons Campsite

Forest trails lead to a famous battlefield.

❶ Leave car park and then follow obvious waymarkers for Loch Trool Trail. Cross bridge over Water of Trool to enter **Caldons Campsite**, then take **L** turn on to footpath that runs along banks of river. Cross over bridge and go past some toilet blocks.

❷ Follow this well waymarked trail through campsite picnic area, across green bridge and then head **R** across grassy area to pick up trail as it heads uphill and into forest.

❸ Keep on this path uphill and through clearing, then go through kissing gate and re-enter woodland. Continue along southern side of **Loch Trool** until you reach interpretation board near loch end. This marks the spot where Robert the Bruce and his army lured the superior English forces to a well-planned ambush and routed them. Using a small part of his force as bait, positioned here, he concealed the bulk of his men on the slopes above. The English were forced to dismount and follow in single file and when they were at their most vulnerable the Scots blocked the path and hurled boulders down on them.

❹ Follow path from here, leaving woodland and heading downhill and to **L**, briefly joining **Southern Upland Way**. Turn **L** and go through two gates and over wooden bridge. Cross bridge over **Gairland Burn** and continue ahead. Eventually reaching bridge over **Buchan Burn**, cross over and take path to **L**, branching off uphill.

❺ Follow this to top and **Bruce's Stone**, which was raised to commemorate victory at the Battle of Glentrool, the first victory in the Independence Wars. From here, look across the clear waters of the loch to the tree-clad hills opposite, which is one of the finest views in Scotland. Follow track past stone then turn **L** on to narrow road, head through car park and keep going until you reach waymarker on **L** which leads to forest trail and take this to return to car park.

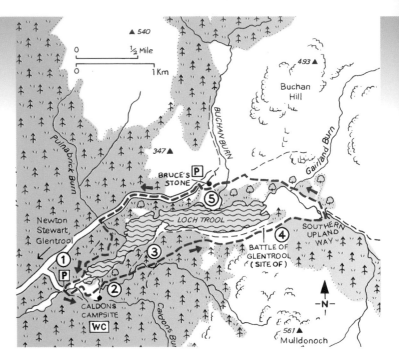

2 Devil's Beef Tub A Hearty Walk

4½ miles (7.2km) 2hrs **Ascent:** 1,076ft (328m)
Paths: Grassy moorlands and firm farm tracks
Suggested map: OS Explorer 330 Moffat & St Mary's Loch
Grid reference: NT 055127
Parking: By forest access gate

Around Devil's Beef Tub near Moffat.

❶ From forest gateway on **A701**, go through wooden gate on **R-H** side, then climb wooden fence ahead. Ascend grassy slope of Annanhead Hill, keeping to **R** of 2 wire fences as you walk to **trig point** on summit.

❷ Bear **R** over **Peat Knowe**, keeping wall and fence to your **L**. Follow path down grassy slope to head of gully, where path meets wall. Walk to other side of gully, then turn **R** and pick your way to edge to enjoy views over **Devil's Beef Tub**.

❸ Follow narrow path as it continues to descend, walking over grass and bracken with valley views. Eventually reach area of pasture, in front of **plantation**. Walk to 2 gates; go through metal gate **R**.

❹ Continue downhill on grassy bank, then go through gate and along rough track, swinging **L** round wall of plantation. Go through gate behind red-brick house, then continue towards farm buildings. Walk between buildings on to tarmac track and towards timber barn, continuing ahead to join farm road.

❺ Follow farm road along valley bottom. Keep an eye out for small area of undulating land on your **R** – it's all that remains of an ancient settlement. Eventually reach **Ericstane** farm.

❻ Turn **R**, through gate, then head uphill on stony track, with woodland on **L**. Soon pass area of pronounced banks and ditches – another reminder of former settlement – then reach house. Shortly after farmhouse, go through gate; turn sharp **R**, following track as it runs by stone wall. Eventually reach main road, cross over (with care) and go through gate.

❼ Continue over **Ericstane Hill**. Bear **R** and follow track north round far side of hill. Track is indistinct in places, covered in grass and reeds. Keep to **L** of summit, walking around brow of hill to rejoin road. Turn **R** here to visit **Covenanter memorial**, or turn **L** to return to start.

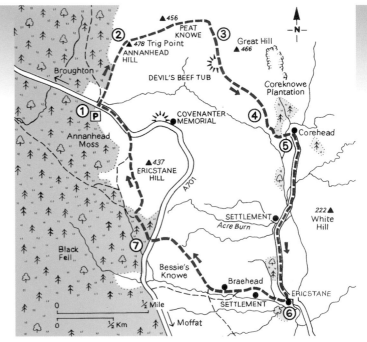

Langholm A Poet's Passions

3 miles (4.8km) 1hr 30min **Ascent:** 919ft (280m)
Paths: Firm hill tracks and tarmac roads
Suggested map: OS Explorer 323 Eskdale & Castle O'er Forest
Grid reference: NY 364845
Parking: On main street in Langholm

An exhilarating climb is followed by a gentle stroll past Hugh MacDiarmid's memorial.

❶ From **post office** on main street, turn **L** and take path next to it that runs uphill. Go through gate at top. Follow grassy track that continues ahead to green seat beside **Whita Well**, natural spring.

❷ Take track just to **L** of seat, running steeply up hill. Follow track as it runs under line of pylons and up to top of **Whita Hill**. Stone steps take you up to the monument, a 100ft (30m) obelisk commemorating Sir John Malcolm, a once-famous soldier, diplomat and scholar. From here you'll get great views – and on a clear day you can see the Lake District peaks.

❸ From monument, walk down few paces to join wide footpath that runs in front of it, then turn **R**. It's easy walking now, following clear track downhill with heather on slopes to either side. Eventually reach unusual metal sculpture on L-H side. The sculpture, which is meant to resemble an open book, was

created by Jake Harvey and is a **memorial** to Hugh MacDiarmid. There's a small cairn there too.

❹ Go through metal gate by sculpture and turn **L**. Now simply follow road as it winds downhill – it's quite a long stretch but it's fairly quiet. Go back under line of electricity pylons then, just after you pass copse on your R-H side, take track on **L**.

❺ Follow this footpath, which is lined with wild grasses and thistles – it's a good place to see butterflies in summer. Eventually footpath becomes less distinct and runs through small boggy patch. After this you soon return to gate that you reached on your outward journey.

❻ Turn **R**, through gate, walk downhill, past golf course and into town. It's quite a steep descent and can be slippery in bad weather. If you're here in summer you should be able to see red clover lining the path, which really attracts bees. Eventually reach main street in **Langholm**, with **hotel** ahead.

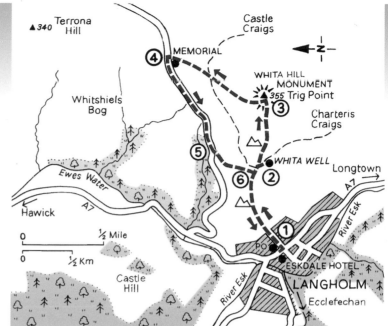

Caerlaverock The Solway Merses

5¼ miles (8.4km) 2hrs 30min **Ascent:** 82ft (25m)
Paths: Country lanes, farm tracks and salt marsh, 1 stile
Suggested map: OS Explorer 314 Solway Firth
Grid reference: NY 051656 **Parking:** Car park at Wildfowl and Wetlands Trust Reserve

An ancient fortress and a nature reserve.

❶ Exit car park and turn **R** on to farm road. Follow this past farms of **Newfield** and **Midtown** then turn **L** and go past bungalow and houses. Just before farm of **Hollands** there is waymarker pointing to car park, on **R**, and straight ahead for walks. Go straight ahead, continue to farm steading and turn **L**.

❷ Go through gate and on to farm track. This stretches into distance and has high hedges on both sides. Continue along this track between hedges and on, over overgrown section, to fence. Cross by stile and turn **R** at signpost ('Caerlaverock National Nature Reserve').

❸ Sign here informs visitors that regulated wildfowling (shooting) takes place between 1 September and 20 February. Follow rough track through grass along edge of **merse** in direction of arrow on footpath waymarker post. Path can be very boggy at all times and grass will be high in summer.

❹ Cross small wooden bridge, electric fence

covered with insulated piping and another small bridge. Path splits at several points and meanders back and forth, but all lines of path rejoin and you'll end up at same place which ever one you take.

❺ Eventually tumbledown wire-and-post fence will appear on R-H side. Follow this fence towards wood, passing through overgrown area and then bear **R**, through gate and into field. Walk to **L** around perimeter of this field, past cottages, and then turn **L** through gate to emerge on to farm track, passing sign pointing way for **Caerlaverock Castle** and into castle grounds.

❻ Follow road past old castle (don't miss information boards) and go through wood with nature trail information boards to **Caerlaverock Castle**.

❼ At far end go through arch and then continue to T-junction with country lane. Turn **R** and continue for about 1 mile (1.6km) then turn **R** on to another lane ('Wildfowl and Wetlands Reserve'). Continue past farms of **Northpark**, **Newmains** and **Nethertown** and then back to car park at **Eastpark**.

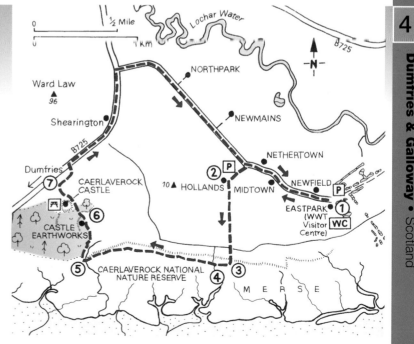

Carsethorn The Solway Shore

5½ miles (8.8km) 2hrs 30min **Ascent:** 82ft (25m) ⚠
Paths: Rocky seashore, woodland tracks and country roads
Suggested map: OS Explorer 313 Dumfries & Dalbeattie, New Abbey
Grid reference: NX 993598
Parking: Car park by beach at Carsethorn

Visit the birthplace of the 'father of the American Navy'.

❶ From car park head down to beach and turn **R**. Continue along shore for 2 miles (3.2km). Beach here is sandy and may be strewn with driftwood, but if tide is in you will be walking over more rocky ground.

❷ After you reach **The House on the Shore**, beside beach on your **R**, headland juts out and you should look for track heading uphill on **R**. At top of hill well-defined track heads alongside stone wall.

❸ Look for fainter track leading off to **L**, which descends steeply to arrive at beach beside natural rock arch called **Thirl Stane**. You can go through the arch to the sea if the tide is in, although if the tide is out, the sea will be far off in the distance.

❹ Continue along rocks on pebble shore and up grassy bank to car park. Exit car park on to lane. Continue on lane past **Powillimount**. Turn **R** at lodge house on R-H side and walk along estate road to cottage birthplace of John Paul Jones.

❺ There are picnic tables here and a **museum**. Continue along road past gates to **Arbigland** on to road ('No vehicular traffic'). Follow road as it turns **R** and along side of Arbigland Estate buildings.

❻ When road turns L at cottage, go **R** on to dirt track. Continue until it emerges on to surfaced road next to **Tallowquhairn** to your **R**. Take road away from farm, turning sharply **L** around houses, then **R** and continue to T-junction.

❼ Turn **R** and follow road round to **L**. Follow long straight road as far as **R** turn to **South Carse**. Go along farm road and straight through farm steading as far as you can, then turn **L**.

❽ To return to shore again, walk along footpath passing brightly coloured caravan and rear of cottages. Look for narrow track heading downhill to **R** allowing access to beach. Turn **L** and walk along beach to car park.

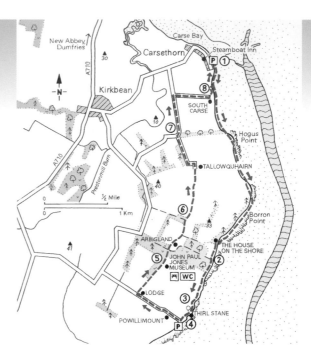

New Abbey To Criffel

3¾ miles (6km) 3hrs **Ascent:** 1,686ft (514m) ⚠
Paths: Forest road, rough hill and wood tracks, 1 stile
Suggested map: OS Explorer 313 Dumfries & Dalbeattie
Grid reference: NX 971634
Parking: Car park at Ardwall farm

The 13th-century love story of the Lady Devorgilla, set forever in stone.

❶ From car park head towards **Ardwall** farm then go through gate on **L**. Turn **R** after 70yds (64m) then head towards hill on track between dry-stone walls. When road curves L, in front of wood, take rough track off to **R**. (Criffel Walk sign has fallen from its post.)

❷ Follow well-trodden track uphill and through trees following course of **Craigrockall Burn**. Path narrows in places and ground is uneven with large boulders to climb over or around. Many trees have been felled here and it is not long before you emerge from woods on to open hillside.

❸ At T-junction with forest road, keep ahead to pick up trail on other side and continue uphill. Ground can be boggy, even in summer, and care needs to be taken. Cross another forest road and eventually reach fence marking where tree line used to be. Cross stile here and veer to **L**, heading towards summit of **Criffel**.

❹ From the OS triangulation pillar on the summit of **Criffel** are views across Solway to the south to England and the hills of the Lake District; a little to the right of that is the Isle of Man, while the coast of Ireland is visible to the west. On good day the summit is an ideal place for a picnic. When you've enjoyed view head roughly northwest from cairn, then go north crossing over rough ground towards broad ridge that runs from **Criffel to** neighbouring hill of **Knochendoch**. When you intersect narrow footpath turn **R**, head downhill on it then continue, ascending again now, to reach summit of **Knochendoch**.

❺ From summit cairn head east and go downhill. In summer, when the heather is particularly thick, the going can be fairly tough and you'll have to proceed slowly and with caution. Make for fence that runs across hill in front of you. Turn **R** here and follow it back to stile. Cross stile and retrace your steps to bottom of hill.

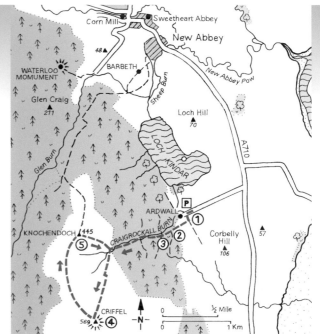

Glenkiln Outdoor Sculptures

4 miles (6.4km) 2hrs 30min **Ascent:** 312ft (95m)

Paths: Country roads, farm tracks, open hillside
Suggested map: OS Explorer 321 Nithsdale & Dumfries
Grid reference: NX 009704
Parking: Car park in front of statue of John the Baptist

Discover works of art in this unique countryside setting.

❶ From car park in front of statue *John the Baptist* return to main road and turn **R**. Cross cattle grid then turn **R** and go past statue to **Marglolly Burn**. Turn **L** and walk along bank towards **Cornlee Bridge**. Just before bridge turn **L** and head back to road. Henry Moore's *Standing Figure* is before you at junction with farm road.

❷ Turn **L** and head back along main road. Just before entrance to **Margreig** farm on R is muddy track running across field to gate in dry-stone wall. Head up and through gate then keep straight ahead, uphill and towards telephone pole. At pole veer **L** and follow track uphill. **Glenkiln Cross** should now be visible ahead.

❸ There are several footpaths and tracks available. Take one that is closest to large tree in front of you. Cross burn at tree then take path that skirts to **L** of it. Veer **R** and head for high ground. Once **cross** comes

into view again head directly towards it.

❹ From **cross** turn to face **Glenkiln Reservoir** then head downhill towards telephone pole. Go through gate in fence at bottom of hill and turn **R** on to road. Short distance along here farm track leads uphill to **R**. Go through gate and on to it. To your R on hillside is Henry Moore's *King and Queen*.

❺ Continue on this track. Go through gate, pass small wooded area on your R and then bare hillside until you spot small stand of Scots pine on your L. Leave road at this point and continue to trees and Epstein's *Visitation*. Return to road and continue to end where you go through gate, over bridge, then turn **L** on to road.

❻ Go downhill for ½ mile (800m), crossing cattle grid. Just before end of conifer plantation on L, look out for Moore's *Two Piece Reclining Figure No 1* on your R. Follow road all way downhill from here, turn **L** at junction and continue to car park.

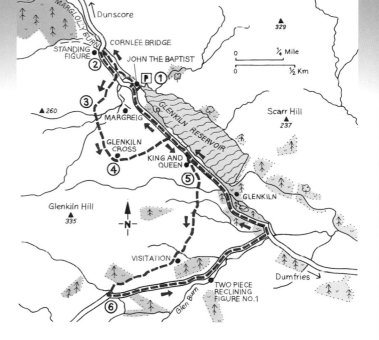

Moniaive The Glasgow Boys

5 miles (8km) 3hrs **Ascent:** 295ft (90m)

Paths: Dirt roads, hill tracks, forest road and country lane
Suggested map: OS Explorers 321 Nithsdale & Dumfries, Thornhill; 328 Sanquhar & New Cumnock, Muirkirk
Grid reference: NX 780910 (on Explorer 328) **Parking:** Moniaive village car park

The village that inspired the Glasgow Boys.

❶ Exit car park and turn **R**. At nearby T-junction turn **R** and go over pedestrian bridge, beside garage, to enter Moniaive High Street at **George Hotel**. Walk along High Street to Market Cross of Moniaive, pass it then turn **L** and cross road. Turn **R** at other side and head up Ayr Street, passing public toilets.

❷ The imposing building on the right with a clock tower is the former village schoolmaster's house. Continue up Ayr Street passing park on R and wooden garages on L. Take next **R** on to narrow lane. Continue to end of lane and, at T-junction turn **R**.

❸ Pass modern bungalow on L, then field, then turn **L** on to dirt road at end of field. Cross bridge and continue up road to **Bardennoch**. When road curves R to enter grounds of house, go straight on and follow road, which goes up side of wood and uphill.

❹ At end of woodland section go through gate and continue uphill on road. Cross fence and then at top,

near ruin of **Upper Bardennoch**, go through another gate. From here continue to climb towards stand of Scots pine, circle them keeping them on your R and continue to summit of **Bardennoch Hill**.

❺ From summit keep going in same direction towards woodland. Wall should be running beside you to R. Head slightly downhill to corner where this wall meets one running in front of woodland. Cross wall and go on to forest road.

❻ Turn **R** and follow road downhill through several gates until it goes through final gate, at T-junction with country lane, where you turn **R**. At next T-junction, L turn will soon take you to hamlet of **Tynron** which is worth visiting. Otherwise turn **R** again.

❼ Follow this road past **Dalmakerran** farm then uphill and through hazel wood. Continue uphill passing cottage on R then, further along, another house. Road starts to go downhill again on to **Dunreggan Brae**. At bottom of hill re-enter **Moniaive**; turn **R** into car park.

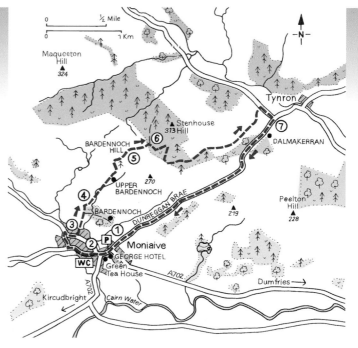

9 Wanlockhead Scotland's Highest Village

3¾ miles (6km) 3hrs **Ascent:** 525ft (160m) 🅐

Paths: Footpaths, hill tracks, hillside and old railway lines, 1 stile

Suggested map: OS Explorer 329 Lowther Hills, Sanquhar & Leadhills

Grid reference: NX 873129

Parking: Museum of Lead Mining car park

Discover the secrets of lead and gold mining.

❶ With museum to your back turn **L** and join **Southern Upland Way**. Head uphill on steps then, at top, cross to stone building with large white door. Turn **R** on to rough road, cross main road and take public footpath to Enterkine Pass. Follow this until you reach the front of white house.

❷ Turn **L** on to an old railway. Follow this, cross road then go through long cutting to fence. Cross stile to **Glengonnar Station** then follow narrow path that runs along **L** side of railway tracks.

❸ Eventually path runs on to rough road and in distance see 2 terraced houses. Where telephone wires intersect road turn **L** at pole on L-H side and follow line of fence down to sheep pens. Turn **R** at end of pens and walk out to main road.

❹ Turn **R** then almost immediately **L** on to hill road. Walk uphill until road bears sharp **R** and dirt track forks **L**. Turn **L** on to track and continue to gate. Cross

over then veer **L** on to faint track. Follow track downhill to where it comes close to corner of fence on your **L**.

❺ Cross fence and go straight ahead on very faint track picking your way through heather. Eventually, as track begins to look more like recognisable path, reach fork. Go **R** and cross flank of hill passing through disused tips.

❻ Path here is little more than series of sheep tracks and may disappear altogether, but don't worry. Ahead is large conical **spoil heap** and, provided you keep heading towards it, you know you will be going in right direction.

❼ Towards end of hill track heads **L**, starts to descend, then passes behind row of cottages. Veer **R**, downhill, after cottages to join road. Turn **L** and continue past **Glencrieff cottages** then turn **R**, leaving road and heading downhill again. Cross bridge and climb up on to **Southern Upland Way**. Turn **L** along it and follow this route back to car park.

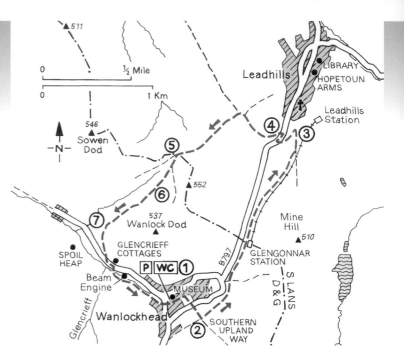

10 Loch Enoch Cycling on the Merrick

9 miles (14.5km) 5hrs **Ascent:** 2,339ft (713m) 🅑

Paths: Hill tracks, section to Loch Enoch can be very boggy, 1 stile

Suggested map: OS Explorer 318 Galloway Forest North

Grid reference: NX 415804

Parking: Bruce's Stone car park

Follow in the cycle tracks of Davie Bell.

❶ From car park at **Bruce's Stone** head east along narrow road, and across **Buchan Bridge**. Continue short distance then turn **L** and go uphill to cross stile. Follow path along wall, then veer **R** and head uphill to rejoin wall. Go through gate and turn **R** on to path. Follow this up valley of **Gairland Burn** with **Buchan Hill** on your **L**.

❷ To your **L** is ridge of **Buchan Hill** and to **R** is **White Brae** and to far side of that is **Rig of the Jarkness**. Do not cross the **Gairland** but keep going on path to reach **Loch Valley**, skirting it to west and then continue beside **Mid Burn** to reach **Loch Neldricken**.

❸ Head for far west corner of loch to find infamous Murder Hole featured by S R Crockett in his novel *The Raiders* (1894). The story is based on a local legend that unwary travellers were robbed on these hills and their bodies disposed of in the loch.

❹ From **Murder Hole** head north, crossing burn and then wall. Pass to east of **Ewe Rig** and tiny **Loch Arron** and eventually reach south side of **Loch Enoch**. Don't worry if the track vanishes or becomes indistinct, just keep heading northwards and you'll eventually reach the loch.

❺ As you approach **Loch Enoch** you will see outline of Mullwarchar beyond it and to **R**. When you reach loch go **L** and then cross another wall. The slope, which is in front of you, is **Redstone Rig** and although you have 1,000ft (305m) to climb it is an enjoyable ascent and not particularly taxing.

❻ From summit cairn of **Merrick** head downhill towards narrow ridge called **Neive of the Spit** to reach summit of **Benyellary**, Hill of the Eagle. From here follow footpath downhill beside dry-stone wall then turn **L** and keep going downhill, into forest, to reach bothy at **Culsharg**. From there continue downhill to return to car park.

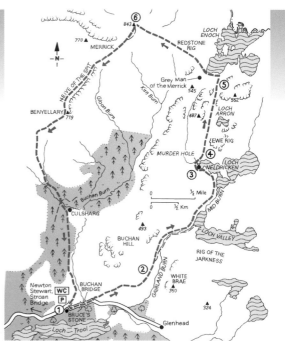

Wigtown The Killing Times

4 miles (6.4km) 3hrs **Ascent:** 98ft (30m)

Paths: Roads, old railway tracks and pavements

Suggested map: OS Explorer 311 Wigtown, Whithorn & The Machars

Grid reference: NX 439547

Parking: At Wigtown harbour

Visit the memorial to two women drowned at the stake for their religion.

❶ Leave car park, turn **R** and head uphill on narrow country lane, Harbour Road. House on L near top of road was former station house for **Wigtown**. Just before it is farm gate on **L**. Go through it and on to farm track.

❷ Follow track to where it goes through another gate then veer **R** and climb up old railway embankment. This has a good grassy surface. Proceed along embankment and through gate.

❸ Wall across track will stop you where former railway bridge carried track across **River Bladnoch**. Turn **R** and go down side of embankment and cross fence into field. Veer **R** and head across field to far corner then go through gate on to main road.

❹ Turn **L** and walk through **Bladnoch**. At junction by roundabout, cross road to enter **Bladnoch Distillery** car park. After visiting distillery head back out of car

park and turn **L** at roundabout. Continue along this road (B7005) for 1 mile (1.6km) to crossroads.

❺ Turn **R** on to B733 and walk along it to **Wigtown**. At centre of town bear **L** round square and head towards large and impressive former county buildings. Pass them on your **R**, then church and war memorial on your **L** and continue downhill. Eventually turn **R** into car park for **Martyrs' Memorial**.

❻ Walk through car park; turn **L** and make your way to bird hide at end of path. From here retrace your steps to car park and continue on path leading to **Martyrs' Memorial**. Turn **L**; walk over sands on wooden causeway to reach the memorial erected to mark the spot where the two women were drowned.

❼ Return to path and turn **L**. Go through kissing gate then another gate, which is slightly below level you are walking on and to **L**. At end of path go through another gate in front of old station house, turn **L** on to Harbour Road and return to car park.

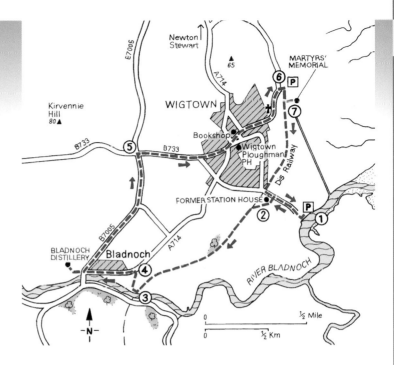

Wells of the Rees Ancient Stone Domes

6¼ miles (10.1km) 3hrs 30min **Ascent:** 558ft (170m)

Paths: Forest roads, forest track, very rough ground

Suggested map: OS Explorer 310 Glenluce & Kirkcowan

Grid reference: NX 260735

Parking: Near Derry farm

A tough walk on the Southern Upland Way.

❶ Cross cattle grid; head west along Southern Upland Way (SUW) on well-surfaced forest road. Pass **Loch Derry**, on R in just under 1 mile (1.6km) then continue on forest road, passing signpost on L to **Linn's Tomb**.

❷ Follow road as it curves **R** and then, following **SUW** markerpost, turn **L**, leave road and head uphill. It's rather steep climb, on fairly well-trodden path with plenty of waymarkers.

❸ Cross forest road and continue on uphill path heading to summit of **Craig Airie Fell**. Reach summit at Ordnance Survey trig point.

❹ From trig point, continue on well-marked path towards waymarker on horizon. Turn **L** at waymarker and head downhill on footpath that twists and turns to another waymarker near bottom. Turn **R** here on to another obvious trail and continue to edge of forest.

❺ **SUW** now follows forest ride. Short distance

along reach clearing with **cairn** on your L-H side. Keep ahead following direction arrows on waymarkers to next clearing where sign points L to **Wells of the Rees**. Turn **L**; head downhill, through bracken, across ruined dry-stone wall, through bracken again and then gap in wall. It is more difficult to find wells in summer, when bracken is thick. First 2 wells are on R as you come through gap and other is off to L.

❻ Retrace your steps from here to signpost and turn **R**. Retrace your steps to edge of forest and turn **R**, following edge of forest and burn, slightly downhill to fence. Cross this and head roughly west across rough and boggy ground towards **Craigmoddie Fell**.

❼ Climb to highest point then look to your L to **Loch Derry** then, to R of it, **Derry** farm. Head in straight line for **Derry** farm then drop down off fell and pick up path heading towards **Loch Derry**.

❽ Follow this to patch of trees, through gate and on to forest road. Turn **R** and return to **Derry farm**.

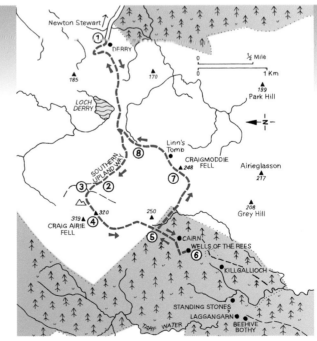

13 Port Logan Fictional Ronansay

2.5 miles (4km) 2hrs **Ascent: 492ft (150m)** ⚠

Paths: Shoreline, country lanes and hill tracks, 1 stile
Suggested map: OS Explorer 309 Stranraer & The Rhins
Grid reference: NX 097411
Parking: Public car park on road to Logan Fish Pond

A walk around a picturesque fishing village where everything is not as it seems.

❶ From car park go across wooden walkway, down some steps on to beach and turn **L** to walk along beach. When you reach start of village climb on to road in front of **Port Logan Inn**. Turn **R** and then continue along main street, passing war memorial to reach **village hall**. In the television series, *Two Thousand Acres of Sky*, the village hall features as a school, and has a school sign fixed to the front. There's also a timetable for Caledonian MacBrayne ferries displayed on the notice-board on the wall. Opposite the village hall is a small but picturesque harbour with a rather unusual lighthouse. Nowadays, when it is not in use as a film location, **Port Logan** harbour is used only by a few pleasure craft.

❷ This was a thriving fishing port in the past and the **pier** once again looks as though it is busy, festooned with fishing gear, gas bottles and sacks of coal.

Although they are all real, they are only there as props. Move away from harbour area and go along road to farm of **Muldaddie**.

❸ Just before farm turn **L** on to old hill track and head uphill. Near the top look back downhill for a magnificent view back to the village and across **Port Logan Bay** to the Mull of Logan. Track is heavily overgrown here, and is blocked by barrier made from gates, but this can easily be crossed by stile at side.

❹ Continue along the track to T-junction.

❺ Retrace your steps to Port Logan then go back on to beach, turn **R** and retrace your steps to car park. From here you can continue along rough road to **Logan Fish Pond**. It's right at the end on **L** and is by the only building there.

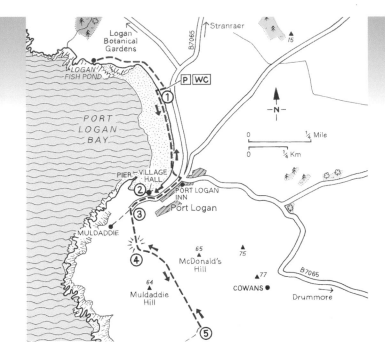

14 Selkirk To the Wilds of Africa

3 miles (4.8km) 1hr 40min **Ascent: 131ft (40m)** ⚠

Paths: Riverside paths and woodland tracks, town streets, 4 stiles
Suggested map: OS Explorer 338 Galashiels, Selkirk & Montrose
Grid reference: NT 469286
Parking: West Port car park in Selkirk

A gentle walk by Ettrick Water, laced with memories of the great explorer Mungo Park.

❶ From Park's statue, walk to Market Place, go **L** down Ettrick Terrace, **L** at church, then sharp **R** down Forest Road. Follow this downhill, cutting off corners using steps, to Mill Street. Go **R**, then **L** on to Buccleuch Road. Turn **R** following signs for riverside walk. Go across **Victoria Park** to join tarmac track.

❷ Turn **L** and walk by river; join road and continue to cross bridge. Turn **L** along Ettrickhaugh Road, passing row of cottages on **L**. Just past them turn **L**. Cross tiny footbridge then take indistinct track on **L**. Walk to river bank. Turn **R**.

❸ Follow path along river margin; it's eroded in places so watch your feet. In spring and summer your way is sprinkled with wild flowers. Eventually join wider track and bear **L**. Follow this until you reach weir and salmon ladder. Turn **R** to cross tiny bridge.

❹ Immediately after this go **L** and continue walking

alongside river until you reach point at which Yarrow Water joins **Ettrick Water**. Retrace your steps for about 100yds (91m) then turn **L** at crossing of tracks.

❺ Your route now goes through woods, then cross bridge by weir again. Take footpath **L**; follow grassy track round meadow until you reach **mill** buildings.

❻ Bear **R** (but don't cross bridge) and continue, walking with mill lade (small canal) on **L**. Where path splits, take track on **L** to follow straight, concrete path beside water to reach **fish farm** (you'll smell it).

❼ Walk around buildings, then bear **L** to continue following mill lade. Go **L** over footbridge, then **R**, passing cottages again. At main road go **R** to reach bridge. Don't cross bridge but join footpath on **L**.

❽ Follow footpath as it goes past sports ground, then skirts housing estate. Continue until you reach pedestrian footbridge on your R-H side, where you cross over river, bear **R**, then retrace your footsteps back over **Victoria Park** and uphill to Market Place.

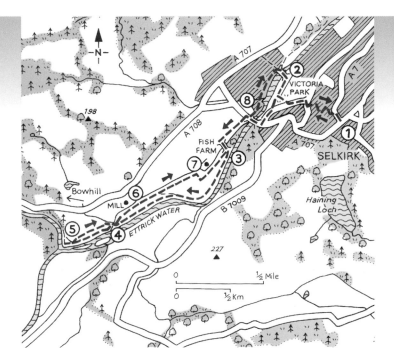

Ettrick Going the Whole Hogg

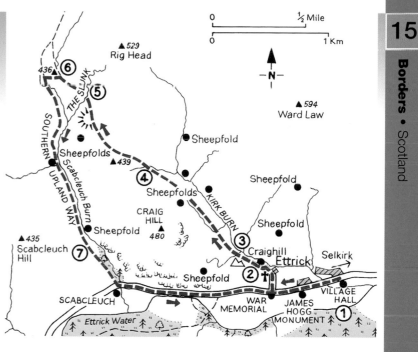

4½ miles (7.2km) 2hrs 30min **Ascent:** 689ft (210m)
Paths: Narrow hill tracks, moorland and waymarked trail, 4 stiles
Suggested map: OS Explorer 330 Moffat & St Mary's Loch
Grid reference: NT 265144
Parking: By village hall on minor road west of B709

In the footsteps of a local poet.

❶ From parking place by village hall, turn **L** along road past **monument to James Hogg** and up to **war memorial**. Turn **R** and walk past church, then take track that bears sharp **L** past farm buildings. Go through metal gate, then fork **L** at right of way sign.

❷ Walk uphill, following track through another gate and up grassy slope. Keep monument on hill above to your **L**. Follow narrow track, passing a circular **sheepfold** on your **L** and 2 on opposite hillside on **R**.

❸ Path now skirts Craig Hill, roughly following **Kirk Burn**. Look for another circular **sheepfold** on your **L**, then 2 more away to **R**. At this point track disappears and ground becomes boggy underfoot. Don't take track that bears **L** but maintain direction, heading for low ground ahead.

❹ Keep walking over moorland – passing lone fence post on your **L**, then circular, stone **sheepfold**, also on L-H side but further away. Continue towards **The Slunk**, heavily eroded burn, from where you get great views back up Ettrick Valley.

❺ Scramble down banks of The Slunk, and cross over water – there are some rocks to help you across, but be careful. Your way then takes you over to meet wire fence. Bear **L** and follow line of fence to metal fingerpost ('Riskinhope').

❻ At fingerpost, cross stile and continue descending along other side of fence to meet **Southern Upland Way**. Cross back over fence at wooden stile, then bear **L** on wide path as it runs back down to Ettrick Valley. Pass 2 well maintained **sheepfolds** along way, and come to stone stile.

❼ Nip over this stile to enter pasture, then go down to meet road at bottom **L-H** corner. Cross another stone stile here and drop into lane opposite **Scabcleuch** farm. Turn **L** again over bridge and walk back to **war memorial**. Walk past **monument** and return to parking place at start.

Newcastleton Remembering the Reivers

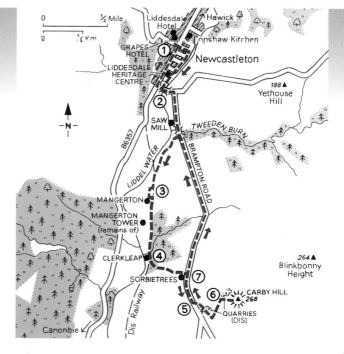

5 miles (8km) 2hrs **Ascent:** 689ft (210m)
Paths: Quiet byroads and farm tracks, one rough climb
Suggested map: OS Explorer 324 Liddesdale & Kershope Forest
Grid reference: NY 483875
Parking: Douglas Square

Through borderlands where cattle raiding was once a part of everyday life.

❶ From Douglas Square, with your back to **Grapes Hotel**, walk along Wyitchester Street (or any other street opposite) and go down to **Liddel Water**. Turn **R**, walk along riverbank and join path downstream to bridge. Turn **L** at top of steps and cross bridge.

❷ After 100yds (91m), turn **R** and follow **Brampton Road**, passing static caravans on either side. Eventually pass old **sawmill** with corrugated iron roof and reach **Tweeden Burn** bridge. Cross bridge and walk uphill, turn **R** and join metalled track that leads to **Mangerton** farm. Continue on this road until you near farm buildings.

❸ Turn **L**, then sharp **R**, and walk down on to bed of old railway line, which has joined you from **R**. Follow line as it leads past remains of **Mangerton Tower**, in a field to your **R**, and continue until you reach **Clerkleap** cottage.

❹ Turn **L** immediately after cottage, then go through wooden gate to join rough track. This leads through woodland and on, uphill, to join road by **Sorbietrees** farm. Turn **R** and walk along road, past farm, to small stand of conifers on **L**. Turn **L** through gate.

❺ Bear **R** now and head up **L-H** side of trees. Walk past top of wood and former **quarry**, to dry-stone wall. Turn **L** and follow wall uphill, crossing it about 437yds (400m) ahead at a convenient R-angle bend.

❻ It's a bit of a scramble now, over bracken and scree, to reach summit – great views. Known locally as **Caerba Hill**, this was once the site of a prehistoric settlement. Retrace your steps to reach road again, then turn **R** and walk back to **Sorbietrees** farm.

❼ At farm, continue on main road as it bears **R** and follow it back over Tweeden bridge and up to Holm Bridge. Cross bridge and walk straight on for 100yds (91m), then turn **R** on to B6357 and walk back to village square via little **heritage centre**.

17

Broughton John Buchan Country

5 miles (8km) 2hrs 30min Ascent: 1,575ft (480m) **3**

Paths: Hill tracks and grassy paths, 1 stile

Suggested map: OS Explorer 336 Biggar & Broughton

Grid reference: NT 119374

Parking: Parking in front of cottage past Broughton Place Art Gallery

A lovely walk through John Buchan country.

1 From parking place, go through gate and follow obvious, grassy track that runs in front of **cottage**. Soon pass a copse on L-H side and then pass **Duck Pond Plantation**, also on L-H side. Track becomes slightly rougher now and you cross wooden rollers to help you over burn.

2 Your track continues ahead, over larger burn and past feathery carpets of heather and bracken – listen for skylarks in summer. Continue walking and path will soon level out and lead you past deep gully on R-H side. Follow track until it bends, after which you come to meeting of tracks.

3 Take track that bears **L** and head for dip that lies between 2 hills – **Clover Law** on L and **Broomy Side** in front. You should just be able to spot fence on skyline. Make for that fence and, as you near it, eventually spot gate, next to which is wooden stile.

4 Cross stile, then turn **R** and follow fence line. You soon get superb views to L. Continue following fence and walk up track until you reach **trig point** on **Broughton Heights** – final ascent's a bit of a puff – but it's thankfully not too long.

5 Now retrace your steps to reach stile again, nip over it, but this time turn **R** and follow narrow track that climbs **Clover Law**. Continue walking in same direction, following fence line as it runs along top of ridge. When you near end of ridge, keep your eyes peeled for track that leads down to your **L**.

6 Follow track as it runs down between 2 **plantations**, roughly in direction of **cottage**, in quite a steep descent. At bottom you come to old wall and burn, which you cross, then continue ahead to reach main track.

7 Turn **R** here and walk past little **cottage** again, through gate and back to your car. If you want to visit **Broughton Place** and its **art gallery**, just continue walking down track to reach house on your L.

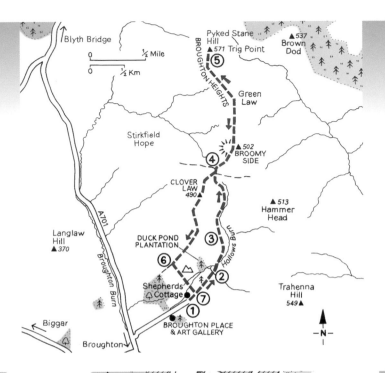

18

Peebles Birthplace of Chambers

3½ miles (5.7km) 1hr 20min Ascent: 295ft (90m) **2**

Paths: Waymarked riverside paths and metalled tracks

Suggested map: OS Explorer 337 Peebles & Innerleithen

Grid reference: NT 250402 **Parking:** Kingsmeadows Road car park, Peebles

Discover the founders of an encyclopaedia on this lovely walk.

1 From Kingsmeadows car park, turn **R** and cross bridge. Turn **L** at **Bridge Hotel** and walk down slope, past swimming pool, to river. Cross small footbridge, go up steps, turn **L** and follow riverside track to pass white bridge and children's play area.

2 Continue following obvious path and cross burn via little bridge, after which path becomes a bit more rugged. Now enter woods, going through kissing gate and following signs ('Tweed Walk'). Eventually leave woods and reach **Neidpath Castle** on R-H side.

3 From castle continue walking by river to go through another kissing gate. Soon come on to higher ground with great view of old railway bridge spanning water in front of you. After another kissing gate, maintain direction to reach red sandstone bridge.

4 Go up to **R** of bridge to join old railway line. Maintain direction and continue following Tweed Walk. Follow this disused track to reach **Manor Bridge**.

5 Turn **L** and cross bridge. Take turning on **L**, ('Tweed Walk'). You're now on metalled track that winds uphill – stop and look behind you for views of Borders landscape, with rolling hills and the busy Tweed. Continue to track on **L** that then leads into woods, ('public footpath to **Peebles** by **Southpark**').

6 Follow this track for few paces, then take wide grassy path which you follow until you leave wood by ladder stile. Follow grassy path downhill, nip over another stile and follow enclosed path – good views of **Peebles** now. Follow obvious track until you join wide tarmac road.

7 Follow road; go **L** into **Southpark Industrial Estate**. Walk to bottom R-H corner past units, then go down steps and bear **L** at bottom. Soon reach footbridge.

8 Turn **R** and follow wide track beside river. This is a popular part of the walk and attracts lots of families on sunny days. Continue walking past weir, then go up steps at bridge and cross over to return to car park.

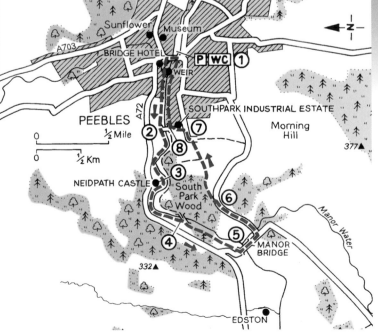

Traquair The Jacobite Rebellion

6½ miles (10.4km) 2hrs 45min **Ascent:** 1,378ft (420m) ▲3
Paths: Firm, wide moorland tracks, 1 stile
Suggested map: OS Explorer 337 Peebles & Inverleithen
Grid reference: NT 331345
Parking: Southern Upland Way car park in Traquair

Jacobite connections in an atmospheric old house and a moorland fairy well.

❶ From **Southern Upland Way** car park, join tarmac road and walk **L** away from **Traquair**. Continue ahead, passing a house called **The Riggs**, and join gravel track following signs for **Minch Moor**. After you go through kissing gate track becomes even grassier, then cross stile and enter Forestry Commission land.

❷ Continue on obvious track to pass **bothy** on R. At crossing of tracks maintain direction, crossing area that has been clear felled. Route goes through gate, just to R of cycle way, winds uphill, through kissing gate and joins up with cycle way again.

❸ Maintain direction, with great views over Walkerburn to L. It feels wilder and windier up here, with large tracts of heather-covered moorland by your path. At marker post, turn **R** and walk up to cairn on **Minch Moor** – views should be great on a clear day.

❹ From cairn, retrace your steps back to main track.

Turn **L** and walk back downhill – stopping to leave some food for the fairies when you pass **Cheese Well** on **L** – it's by boggy part of path. Continue, to go through gate again, to reach next crossing of tracks.

❺ Turn **L** and walk downhill. Landscape opens out on R-H side giving pleasant views of valley and river winding away. At apex of bend, turn **R** along grassy track. Follow this downhill, go through gate and walk in front of **Camp Shiel** cottage.

❻ Go through another gate, cross burn, then follow grassy track and pass **Damhead Shiel** cottage. Go through another gate and follow path across bridge over burn. Pass expanse of scree on R-H side, and ox-bow lake evolving on L. Cross bridge and continue to **Damhead** farm.

❼ Walk past farm and down to road, turn **R**. Now cross burn again and walk past cottages on R-H side. When you reach war **memorial** on L, turn **R** and walk up track to reach parking place at start of walk on L.

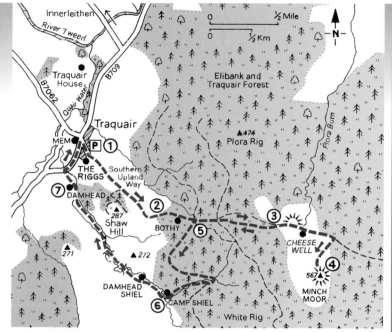

Jedburgh Holy Orders

4½ miles (7.2km) 3hrs **Ascent:** 295ft (90m) ▲2
Paths: Tracks, meadow paths and some sections of road, 2 stiles
Suggested map: OS Explorer OL16 The Cheviot Hills
Grid reference: NT 651204
Parking: Main car park by tourist information centre

Pathways from a historic town.

❶ From car park, walk back to **A68**. Turn **R**, then cross over before river. Take path on **L** to walk beside river, under old bridge, then come on to road. Cross and join road opposite. Take 1st **R** turn, then turn **R** at fire station and cross bridge.

❷ Turn **L**, following sign for **Borders Abbeys Way**. Where road divides, turn **L** and walk beside river again – there's a small 'W' waymarker. At main road, cross over and walk along tarmac road. Continue to large building on your **L** (derelict at time of writing).

❸ Turn **R** here to walk in front of farmhouse, **Woodend**. At another tarmac road, turn **L**. Route now runs uphill, taking you past radio **mast** and in front of **Mount Ulston** house. Maintain direction to join narrow grassy track – can be very muddy, even in summer.

❹ Squelch along track to fingerpost at end, where you turn **L** to join **St Cuthbert's Way** – wide, firm track. At tarmac road, turn **R** and join main road. Turn

L, go over bridge, then cross road and go down steps to continue following **St Cuthbert's Way**.

❺ You're now on narrow, grassy track beside river. Cross couple of stiles before walking across meadow frequently grazed by sheep. Walk past **weir**, then go through gate to cross suspension bridge – take care as it can get extremely slippery.

❻ Pass sign for **Monteviot House** and then walk through woods to fingerpost, where you can turn **R** to enjoy views over river. To extend your walk, continue along **St Cuthbert's Way** until it joins road, then retrace your steps. Whatever you choose, you then retrace your steps back over suspension bridge, along riverside and back to main road. Cross over and rejoin tarmac track.

❼ Track almost immediately forks and you now turn **R**, following road to join **A68** once again. Turn **L** and follow road back into **Jedburgh**. Eventually you'll come to car park on L-H side.

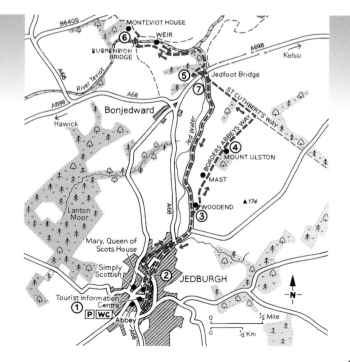

Dryburgh A Great Scott

4½ miles (7.2km) 1hr 30min Ascent: 131ft (40m) ⚠

Paths: Firm woodland and riverside tracks, 3 stiles

Suggested map: OS Explorer 338 Galashiels, Selkirk & Melrose

Grid reference: NT 592318

Parking: Dryburgh Abbey car park

A gentle walk in the Borders countryside much beloved by Sir Walter Scott.

❶ From car park at **abbey** walk back to join road, pass entrance to **Dryburgh Abbey Hotel**, then walk down road in front of you. You'll soon see river and will then pass small **temple** in trees on R-H side. Go **L** and cross bridge over **River Tweed**.

❷ Turn **L** immediately and then join **St Cuthbert's Way**. This waymarked trail now takes you along banks of river. At some points there are steps, tiny footbridges and patches of boardwalk to assist you. Continue to follow this trail which eventually takes you past 2 small islands in river, where it then leads away from river bank.

❸ Follow trail on to a tarmac track, bear **R** and then **L**. At main road in **St Boswells** go **L** again and continue to follow trail signs, passing **post office** and later Scott's View chippy on **L**. After house No 101, turn **L** then go to your **R** along a tarmac track at end.

❹ Follow this, then turn **L** and walk past golf **club house**. Continue few paces, then turn **R** and follow **St Cuthbert's Way** as it hugs golf course. Continue by golf course until your track eventually brings you back down to river bank. Walk past **weir** and up to bridge.

❺ Go up steps and cross bridge, then turn sharp **L** and walk towards cottages. Before cottages, go **L**, over footbridge, then turn **R** along river bank to walk in front of them. At **weir**, take steps that run up to **R**, nip over stile and into field.

❻ Go **L**, through gate, and follow indistinct track overgrown with high grasses in summer, but isn't hard to follow. Where path divides, go **L** to keep to river, now you'll be on short, springy grass.

❼ Follow river, keeping an eye out for fish leaping up to feed from the water's surface. You'll cross stile, then pass greenhouse on your **L**. Climb another stile here, turn **R**, walk past toilets and, at house ahead, turn **L** and walk back into car park.

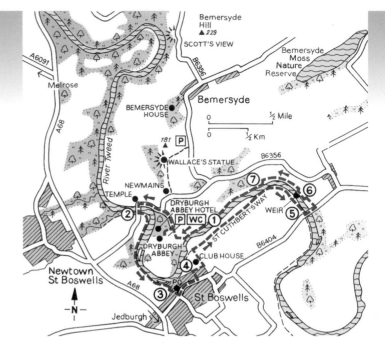

Kirk Yetholm Over the Border

5 miles (8km) 3hrs 45min Ascent: 1,378ft (420m) ▲

Paths: Wide tracks and waymarked paths, one short overgrown section, 3 stiles

Suggested map: OS Explorer OL16 The Cheviot Hills

Grid reference: NT 839276

Parking: Car park outside Kirk Yetholm at junction of Pennine Way and St Cuthbert's Way

An energetic walk over the Scottish border.

❶ From car park cross bridge, following signs ('St Cuthbert's Way'). Follow track uphill, keeping **Shielknowe Burn** below on **L**. Eventually track crosses burn, then continues uphill, skirting edge of **Green Humbleton** hill, eventually reaching fingerpost.

❷ Here, **St Cuthbert's Way** splits from **Pennine Way**. Take **L-H** track, **St Cuthbert's Way**, narrow grassy sheep track. Continue uphill, to fingerpost by wall marking border between Scotland and England.

❸ Follow track which eventually bears downhill to boggy area. Look out for waymarkers, then continue to wood. Cross stile and into trees. Maintain direction, turn **R** at fence and follow fence line. Soon walk down avenue of trees and leave wood by stile.

❹ Keep ahead over field, then descend to cross burn and join wider track. Eventually reach **Elsdonburn** farm. Walk through farm and follow track as it bears **R**. Join track with wood **L** and burn **R**.

❺ Continue, crossing cattle grid, then leave **St Cuthbert's Way**; join track on **R**. Continue, pass **sheepfold** then 2 conifer plantations. Finally, track winds upwards, skirts hill, then descends to **Trowupburn** farmhouse. Walk in front of farm buildings; bear **R** to fingerpost.

❻ Go through gate and follow sign ('Border Ridge 1½'). Continue on this wide grassy track then cross **ford** next to very large **sheepfold**. Maintain direction, burn now on **R**, then cross burn again, cross stile and join sheep track that bears **L** through bracken.

❼ Walk round hill and, when parallel with **sheepfold** on **L**, bear **R** so valley of **Wide Open** burn is on your **L**, **sheepfold** behind you. Continue uphill through bracken to head of burn to fence on higher ground.

❽ Go through gate at corner; cross open ground. Descend to cross burn and keep ahead, crossing border. Bear **R** on **Pennine Way**. At fingerpost follow track downhill and cross burn to start.

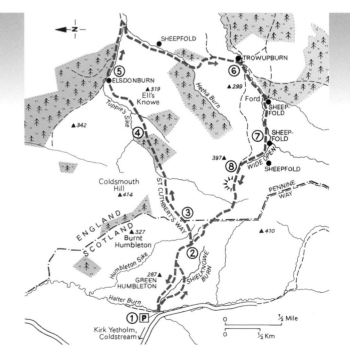

St Abbs A Windy Walk

4 miles (6.4km) 1hr 30min **Ascent:** 443ft (135m)
Paths: Clear footpaths and established tracks
Suggested map: OS Explorer 346 Berwick-upon-Tweed
Grid reference: NT 913674
Parking: At visitor centre

A refreshing walk along the cliffs where there is plenty of wildlife.

❶ From car park, take path that runs past information board and play area. Continue past **visitor centre** and then take footpath on your **L**, parallel to main road. At end of path turn **L** and then go through kissing gate – you'll immediately get great views of the sea.

❷ Follow track, pass sign to **Starney Bay** and continue, passing fields on your L-H side. Your track now winds around edge of bay – to your **R** is little harbour at **St Abbs**. The track then winds around cliff edge, past dramatic rock formations and eventually reaching some steps.

❸ Walk down steps, then follow grassy track as it bears **L**, with fence on **L**. Go up slope, over stile and maintain direction on obvious grassy track. Path soon veers away from cliff edge, past high ground on **R**, then runs up short, steep slope to crossing of tracks.

❹ Maintain direction by taking **L-H** track which runs up slope. You'll soon get great views of St Abb's Head **lighthouse** ahead, dramatically situated on the cliff's edge. Continue to lighthouse and walk in front of **lighthouse** buildings and down to join tarmac road.

❺ Follow this road which takes you away from cliff edge. Continue to obvious bend, from where you get your first views of **Mire Loch** below. You now follow path downhill to right, to reach cattle grid.

❻ Turn **L** here to pick up narrow track by loch, with wall on your R-H side. It's pretty overgrown at start so it can be hard to find, but as you continue it becomes much more obvious. Walk beside loch and continue until you reach gate.

❼ Turn **R** along wide track and walk up to road. Go **L** now and continue to cross cattle grid. When you reach a bend in road, follow tarmac track as it bears **L**. You'll soon go through a gate, then pass some cottages before reaching car park on L-H side.

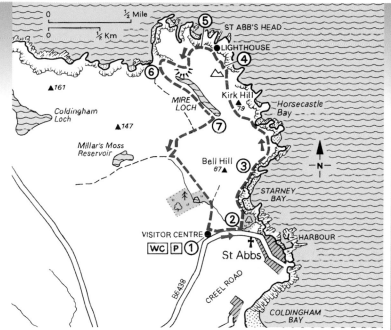

Roslin Romantic Roslin Glen

5 miles (8km) 2hrs 30min **Ascent:** 279ft (85m)
Paths: Generally good, but can be muddy and slippery
Suggested map: OS Explorer 344 Pentland Hills
Grid reference: NT 272627
Parking: Roslin Glen Country Park car park

Tree-lined paths take you beside a river to a special ancient chapel in this glorious glen.

❶ From **country park** car park, walk northeast on to track to reach river. Go up metal stairs, cross footbridge, then walk ahead, following path uphill. In summer, you'll smell wild garlic. At bottom of flight of steps, turn **R**, walk under old **castle** arch, down stone steps, then turn to your **L**.

❷ Your path now descends and you keep walking ahead, before climbing more steps. Path ascends again, until you reach crossing of paths where you turn **R** and follow path steeply downhill. Keep going down until you reach water's edge.

❸ Walk to your **L**, then follow path as it climbs again (handrail to assist you). At crossing of paths turn **R**, following direction of river. Your way now takes you high above river; continue ahead to cross stile. After you cross another stile view opens out to fields on your **L**, then takes you closer to river again. Cross burn and

another stile to point where river goes back on itself.

❹ Cross broken fence, then keep ahead, passing old pollarded tree on L-H side. Follow small sign pointing uphill to **Maiden Castle**. At top turn **L** ('caution, path erosion'). You now get great views over river valley as you cross over ridge and then keep walking to reach a metal gate.

❺ Turn **L** and follow wide path. Eventually pass buildings of **Animal Research Centre**, then pass **memorial** to Battle of Rosslyn on your R-H side. Keep ahead, through outskirts of **Roslin** and up to crossroads at village centre.

❻ Turn **L** and walk ahead. After short distance you see **Rosslyn Chapel** on R-H side. If you don't intend to visit chapel, take path that bears downhill to **R**, just in front of it. When you reach cemetery turn **L** ('Polton'), and walk between cemeteries to metal gate for **Rosslyn Castle**. Go down steps on R-H side, over bridge again and return to car park.

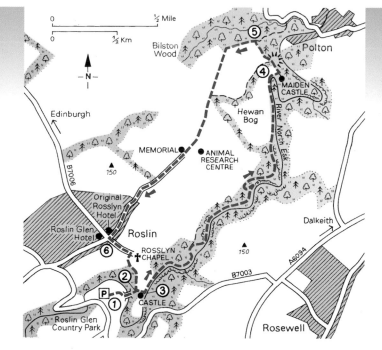

25 East Linton Poppy Harvest

4½ miles (7.2km) 2hrs 30min **Ascent:** 295ft (90m)
Paths: Field paths, river margins and woodland tracks. Short section of busy road, 2 stiles
Suggested map: OS Explorer 351 Dunbar & North Berwick
Grid reference: NT 591772
Parking: Main street in East Linton

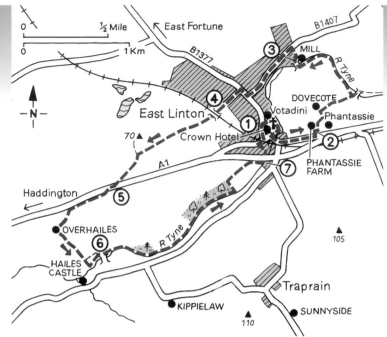

A lovely walk past an old doo'cot and a mill.

1 From Market Cross in centre of town, take path that runs to **L** of church. At main street bear **L**, cross over bridge and continue to garage on R-H side. Turn **L** into farm opposite garage ('Houston Mill and Mill House').

2 Follow path round farm buildings to old doo'cot (**dovecote**) ahead. Turn **R** front of it and follow path along field edge. At footbridge, turn **L** to continue walking around field edge, with river on **R**. Cross next footbridge and go through metal gate.

3 Take **R-H** path across field and go through kissing gate to old **mill**. Inspect **mill** — you can go inside when it's open — continue on to meet main road, then turn **L** back into town. Turn **R** along High Street, cross road and turn **L** to go down Langside.

4 At recreation ground, maintain direction and walk towards railway. Go through underpass and walk ahead through fields. Continue in same direction,

crossing 3 walls with help of steps and 2 stiles. After you cross 3rd wall track becomes indistinct, but maintain direction to reach wooden sign. Turn **L** here to reach road.

5 Turn **R**, cross over at parking place to continue along track running parallel to road. Walk to **Overhailes** farm, through yard, then bear **L** and follow wide track down to **Hailes Castle**. Ignore 1st path that joins from **L** and go a few paces further to turn **L** along another path that leads to bridge.

6 Don't cross bridge but instead follow track that runs to **L** of steps. You're now walking along river's edge on narrow path. Follow path to cross stile, walk along field margin, then enter woods. Ascend flight of stairs, go down steps, and continue following path to walk under road bridge.

7 Path runs through garden and on to road, where you turn **R**. Walk under railway bridge, turn **L** and return to starting point of walk in town.

---

26 Ballantrae Ardstinchar Castle

3 miles (4.8km) 2hrs **Ascent:** 295ft (90m)
Paths: Country lanes and farm tracks
Suggested map: OS Explorer 317 Ballantrae, Barr & Barrhill
Grid reference: NX 082824 **Parking:** Car park near school on Foreland, Ballantrae

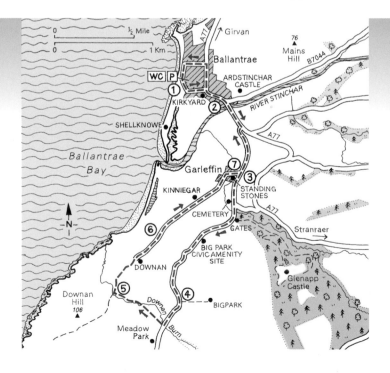

The Ayrshire Tragedy, a murder most foul.

1 Leave car park and then turn **L** on to Foreland. At T-junction with Main Street cross road and turn **R**. Near outskirts of village, just before bridge over **River Stinchar**, look to **L** to view ruins of **Ardstinchar Castle**. Walls are unstable, do not go closer.

2 From here cross Stinchar Bridge and take 1st turning on **R**, heading uphill on narrow country lane and past cottages. At junction keep to **L** but look out for one of **Garleffin Standing Stones** in rear garden of bungalow at junction.

3 Continue uphill passing **cemetery**, **R**, **Glenapp Castle gates** on **L** and further on **Big Park Civic Amenity Site**, on **L**.

4 Continue past farm road to **Bigpark** on **L** and look out for next farmhouse on **R**. About 300yds (274m) before this house road dips; there's stream beside road here. Turn **R** on to farm track that heads downhill between 2 high hedges.

5 Near bottom of hill, just past large barn on **L**, road

splits. Turn **R** and continue along road, through farm steading, past **Downan** farmhouse and uphill. When road levels out look to horizon ahead for distinctive outline of Knockdolian Hill, referred to by local mariners as 'false Craig'.

6 Look over to your **L** at same time to see real Ailsa Craig away to northwest. Looking along beach towards **Ballantrae** is **Shellknowe**. Continue along this road, past farm of **Kinniegar** and through hamlet of **Garleffin**. Note that some houses have names like Druidslea and Glendruid.

7 In front garden of Druidslea is another **standing stone**. Turn **L**, go downhill on country lane, turn **L** on to main road and return to **Ballantrae**. Go through gate on L-H side and into **kirkyard**. Kennedy crypt can be found by going up some steps on **R**. If door is locked look through small window on door. Return to Main Street and turn **R**, go along street and take 1st turning **L** past library. Walk along street to T-junction and turn **L** into Foreland and return to car park.

Byne Hill Firth of Clyde

3¾ miles (6km) 3hrs **Ascent:** 571ft (174m)
Paths: Farm roads, dirt tracks and open hillside, 1 stile
Suggested map: OS Explorer 317 Ballantrae, Barr & Barrhill
Grid reference: NX 187955
Parking: On road beside Girvan cemetery

Enjoy the views across the sea to Ailsa Craig.

1 Go along road to **Brochneil** farm which runs along east side of **cemetery**. Continue through Brochneil steading, then cross wooden bridge. Go through gate, over stone bridge and follow road uphill, as it turns **R**, and then **L**.

2 This is farm road to **Drumfairn**, formerly shepherd's house for Woodland farm, now part of wildlife reserve. Cross cattle grid, go through 2 gates then, at 3rd cattle grid, cross stile and go **L** towards **Drumfairn** steading.

3 The house at Drumfairn has been damaged by fire, is derelict and in a dangerous condition. Turn **R** at steading and, keeping sheep pens on your **L**, walk ahead. Go through gate and then cross wire fence near another gate. Go through this gate and head **R**, across field. At fence turn **L** and follow it to reach junction with tumbledown wall. Cross here and, keeping fence on your **R**, head along edge of field.

Cross small burn near sheep pens and continue following line of fence to gate.

4 Go through gate then go **R**, cross small burn and continue along faint track heading for saddle between **Mains Hill** on your L-H side and **Byne Hill** on your R. Retrace your steps short distance and turn **L** through gap in wall and head up side of **Byne Hill** to prominent commemorative **cairn** at summit. On a clear day you can see the Antrim coast of Northern Ireland, the island of Arran and the Mull of Kintyre to the north and west, and, about 8 miles (12.9km) out in the sea, the distinctive outline of Ailsa Craig, the plug of an extinct volcano and source of granite for curling stones.

5 With **cairn** at your back, walk ahead. Cross saddle between summit and lower part of hill, keeping at first to higher ground then descending towards northeast side of hill where footpath ends at kissing gate. Go through this gate and turn **L** on to farm road. Retrace your steps from here to return to start.

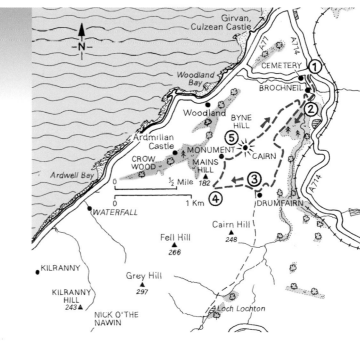

Loudoun Lady Flora

7½ miles (12.1km) 4hrs **Ascent:** 187ft (57m)
Paths: Pavements, footpaths and farm roads
Suggested map: OS Explorer 334 East Kilbride Galston & Darvel
Grid reference: NS 539373 **Parking:** On-street parking near Lady Flora's Institute

A tragic tale of jealousy and intrigue.

1 From Lady Flora's Institute, go south along Main Street. Turn **L** into Craigview Road. Cross bridge, turn **R** and follow road to T-junction. Turn **L** then, where road forks, keep to **R**, go along side of factory, turn **L** into Stonygate Road. Continue to join Irvine Footpath.

2 Continue, passing **Strath** and on to kennels. Turn **R** at gate; follow path round perimeter. Continue along river bank on muddy path. Keep on this, going through woodlands until you see white cottage.

3 As path forks go **L** through gap stile on to surfaced road heading to **L** of **Barr Mill**, and uphill to main road. Continue, heading downhill and passing Galston library, Barr Castle Social Club and Masons Arms pub to crossroads –'Four Corners'.

4 Turn **R**, cross road and continue, heading out of town, crossing 'Muckle Brig' and **Galston** bypass to pavement; continue along A719 towards **Loudoun Academy**. Pass **Waterside** farm on L, **academy** on R then entrance gates to **Loudoun Castle**.

5 Turn **L** opposite gates and head along narrow country lane for ½ mile (800m) to **Loudoun Kirk** Bridge. Turn **L**; go into Loudoun kirkyard. Return from there, cross small bridge and turn **R** on to signposted footpath ('Galston'). After 100yds (91m) path bends R and narrow grassy footpath forks L. Go **L**.

6 Keep on well-trodden path to T-junction at **Galston** bypass. Turn **R**. Head along pavement, over bridge then turn **R** and head downhill. Turn **L** at waymarker and go through underpass to other side of bypass. Turn **L**. Walk along footpath beside river.

7 At end of path go **R** on lane then **L** into Titchfield Street. Turn **R** at next junction, cross road; take next **L**. Pass school and **cemetery** to reach staggered junction. Cross B7037. Continue on Clockstone Road.

8 Turn **L** at T-junction. Take next **R** beside house. Follow road downhill, then back up to pass **Piersland** farm. Head downhill and cross gate where road turns **L** under railway bridge. Turn **R** after bridge; retrace your steps to start.

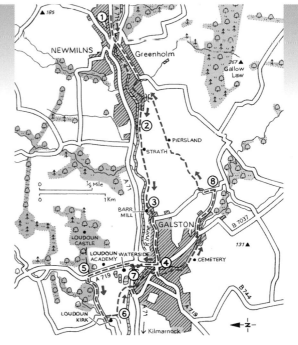

29 Dunaskin The Iron Works

4 miles (6.4km) 3hrs Ascent: 492ft (150m)
Paths: Old rail and tram beds and rough hillside
Suggested map: OS Explorer 327 Cumnock & Dalmellington
Grid reference: NX 440084
Parking: Dunaskin Open Air Museum

A hill walk to a deserted village.

❶ Turn **R** in front of **visitor centre**. Follow road towards **playground**. Go uphill on track to **R** of **playground** and through woodland. Emerge at T-junction opposite railway bridge; turn **L** on grassy trail.

❷ At metal gate across trail, go through small wooden one at its side. Climb over next gate, turn **R** and head uphill following line of disused **tramway**, between ends of an old bridge. This is trackbed of former horse-drawn **tramway**.

❸ At top of hill, when path divides, keep **L** and follow path as it goes through 2 short sections of wall. Ground to your **R** in front of conifer plantation was once village football field. Where path is blocked by fence, turn **R**, then go **L** through gate and **R** on to metalled lane.

❹ Head along here, past remains of miners' houses of **Step Row**, which are clearly visible amongst trees. Stone **memorial** stands near site of former village

store. To **R** of this, and now within wood, is former village square and remains of more houses.

❺ From stone **memorial** turn back towards **war memorial**, then return to gate at corner of wood and continue along track beside wood. In trees are remains of **Low Row**. Go through another gate and continue along former railway. When it forks, keep **R**.

❻ Continue until route ahead is blocked by sheets of corrugated iron, near wall. Turn **R** and follow line of wall downhill. Cross wall and continue downhill towards **chimneys of Dunaskin**. At broken hedge, near end of **Green Hill**, turn **R** along front of it and continue until you are level with 2nd **chimney**.

❼ Turn **L**, heading downhill short way then though gate. Veer to **R** and head towards wooded area. Go through wood and emerge at **Ardoon**. Go past house, turn **L** on to footpath and follow it downhill and under small, disused railway bridge. Cross track and carry on heading back downhill on footpath back to start.

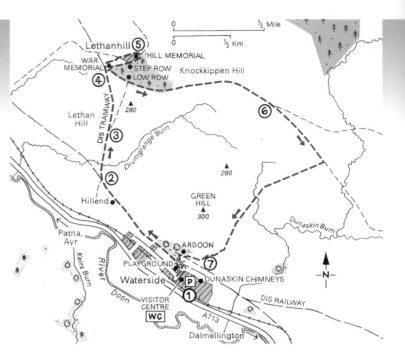

30 Muirkirk On Old Roads and Rails

3½ miles (5.7km) 3hrs Ascent: 16ft (5m)
Paths: Old railway beds, farm tracks and country lanes, 1 stile
Suggested map: OS Explorer 328 Sanquhar & New Cumnock
Grid reference: NX 696265
Parking: Walkers' car park, Furnace Road

Around a once prosperous moorland town that stood at an industrial crossroads.

❶ From car park follow blue waymarker and exit via gate on to rough track with high wall running along to **R**. This continues as fence and, once past end of it, look for waymarker pole on **L**.

❷ Turn **L** on to grass track. Follow this to steps, go downhill and through kissing gate. Turn **R** and walk along what may have been bank of 18th-century canal. Go through kissing gate then veer **L** on to rough track at next waymarker.

❸ Follow to duckboard and stile; cross here. Turn **L** on to gravel path; turn **R** at waymarker. Railway track here appears to fork. Keep **L** and continue along trackbed eventually reaching kissing gate.

❹ Go through gate and turn **R** on to quiet country road. Follow this past remains of old railway bridge, past farm entrance on **R** then go through gate to continue on farm road. At next gate turn **R**, go through

4 gates and return to car park.

❺ Turn **R** and exit car park on to Furnace Road then turn **L**. Continue past clock tower of derelict **Kames Institute** and along edge of **golf course**. Go through gate and continue, passing cottage on **L**, on to old drove road to Sanquhar. Go through another gate and continue to **McAdam memorial**.

❻ Just past this head along green track on **R**. When it forks **L** on to what may have been a tramline, keep **R**. Follow this track along side of stream until it joins dirt track just above **Tibbie's Brig**. Near here, in a small clay dwelling, lived local poetess, Tibbie Pagan, who eked out a living by singing, selling her poetry and possibly supplying illicit whisky. A volume of her poems was published in 1803.

❼ Go down to **Brig** and **monument** then return uphill keeping **L** on access for disabled route to McAdam's cairn. Follow this back to drove road where you turn **L** to return to car park.

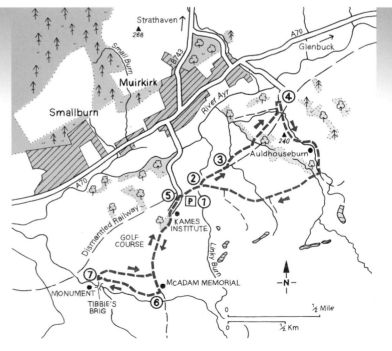

Darvel Sir Alexander Fleming

7 miles (11.3km) 3hrs **Ascent:** 459ft (140m)

Paths: Country lanes and pavements
Suggested map: OS Explorer 334 East Kilbride, Galston & Darvel
Grid reference: NX 563374
Parking: On-street parking at Hastings Square at start of walk

In the footsteps of Sir Alexander Fleming.

❶ From Alexander Fleming Memorial, cross square to pedestrian crossing, cross road, turn **R** and go along Main Street. Near outskirts of town cross Darvel Bridge and take 2nd turning on **L** just past **John Aird Factory**. Go uphill on this road and pass cemetery.

❷ Continue uphill to crossroads near **New Quarterhouse** farm. Follow waymark arrow pointing **L**. Road continues uphill, passing **Henryton** on R and **Byres** on L. Near **Byres** there is a bench if you want some respite on this steep climb.

❸ **Little Glen** is next farm on L-H side and shortly afterwards road forks. Take **L** turn. Next 2 farms passed on this road are **Meikleglen** and **Feoch**, which come in quick succession. Just before next farm on L, **Laigh Braidley**, farm road leads off to R. This is the entrance to Lochfield, Alexander Fleming's birthplace, which is not open to the public. Continue past **Laigh Braidley**.

❹ After **Laigh Braidley** road turns sharply **L**, then **R** and goes downhill to cross Glen Water at **Braidley Bridge**. As you descend hill look slightly to R and uphill and you will see steading of Lochfield, which is still farmed. Follow road uphill from bridge. There's another bench by the roadside at the T junction near the top of hill. Enjoy a well-earned rest and the view.

❺ Ignore waymark and turn **L**, heading along lane and past **Gateside**. When road forks take **L** fork, cross **Mucks Bridge** and continue uphill. Lane now passes roads to **Low** then **High Carlingcraig**, then levels out. As you continue along top of this hill look to L for distinctive outline of Loudoun Hill.

❻ When you reach **Dyke**, road heads downhill again. Go over crossroads at **Intax** and continue short distance to bungalows on R. Just past here take **L** turn. After Hilltop road turns sharply **R** and downhill. As you approach town lane continues into Burn Street. At T-junction turn **L**; follow it back to Hastings Square.

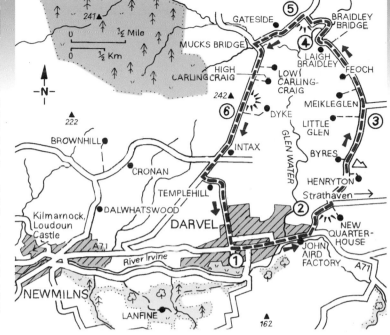

New Lanark A Revolutionary Utopia

6 miles (9.7km) 3hrs **Ascent:** 476ft (145m)

Paths: Clear riverside tracks and forest paths, a few steep steps
Suggested map: OS Explorer 335 Lanark & Tinto Hills
Grid reference: NS 883426
Parking: Main car park above New Lanark

A rustic walk from a model community.

❶ From car park, walk downhill into **New Lanark**. Bear **L** and walk to Scottish Wildlife Trust **visitor centre**. Turn up stone steps on **L** ('Falls of Clyde'). Path soon goes down some steps to reach **weir**, where you'll find lookout point.

❷ Continue along path. You'll pass Bonnington **Power Station** on your R, where it divides. Take **R-H** path, which begins to climb and takes you into woodland and up some steps. You'll soon come to **Corra Linn** waterfall, with another lookout point.

❸ Your path continues to R ('Bonnington Linn', ¾ miles). Go up some more steps and follow track to go under double line of pylons. You'll pass an area that is often fenced to protect breeding peregrines. Follow path to reach large new bridge, cross it, then turn **R** into Falls of Clyde **Wildlife Reserve**.

❹ Walk through reserve, turn **R** at crossing and over small bridge. Pass underneath double line of pylons again, then bear **R** at gate to reach **Corra Castle**. Continue walking by river, cross small footbridge, then follow wide path through woods. When you meet another path, turn **R**.

❺ Follow path to pass houses on your L. At road turn **R** (take care, no pavement), then **R** again to cross old bridge, which brings you into cul de sac. Go through gate on **R** – it looks like someone's drive but is signed ('Clyde Walkway').

❻ Walk past stables to river. Go through gate to water treatment works, up steps beside it, then pass stile on your L. Continue on main track ('Clyde Walkway'). Pass house on R and follow path leading down to **R** (you'll see broken fingerpost there).

❼ Your path zig-zags down to river. At water's edge turn **L**, cross footbridge and follow forest track. Go down some steps, close to river again, then up more steps and over bridge. Follow path to road, turn **R** and into **New Lanark**. Turn **L** at church for car park.

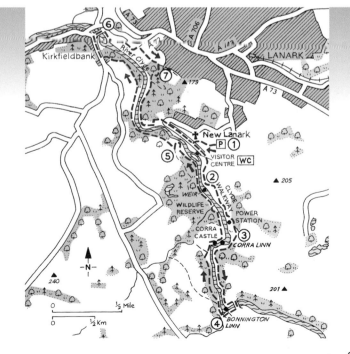

33 East Kilbride Kittochside Farm

5 miles (8km) 3hrs **Ascent:** 262ft (80m)

Paths: Farm tracks and country roads
Suggested map: OS Explorer 342 Glasgow
Grid reference: NS 608558
Parking: Car park at Museum of Scottish Country Life

An 18th-century time warp in a 20th-century new town.

❶ Exit car park and turn **R** on to road, heading past front of main Exhibition Building, then turn **R** on to farm road. Continue along this, keeping your eyes open for tractors ferrying visitors from Exhibition Building to farm. Take gated turn off to **L** and follow this path to go through another gate on to farm road.

❷ Turn **L** and, short distance further on, turn **R** on to another farm road. Follow this across field and into wooded area surrounding **Wester Kittochside**. Road turns sharply **R** then joins another road. Turn **L**, walk past bungalow then turn **L** again where farm road joins country road.

❸ Follow this quiet road for just over 1 mile (1.6km), past fields of **Wester Kittochside** farm, then fields of more modern farms and finally into **Carmunnock**. Road ends at T-junction. Turn **R** then, short distance further on, take next turning on **R** into **Cathkin Road**.

❹ Keep on **Cathkin Road** for about ½ mile (800m) then, when it bends sharply to **L**, turn **R** and continue straight ahead on minor road. Follow this as it twists and turns to reach **Highflat Farm** after about ½ mile (800m) and then continues for another ½ mile (800m) to end at T-junction opposite road leading to **West Rogerton** farm.

❺ Turn **R** and, in just over ½ mile (800m), you will come to crossroads. On **R** is farm track leading back to **Highflat**. Turn **L** here and proceed to next T-junction. Walk along this country lane passing farm of **East Kittochside** on **L**.

❻ Pass junction on your **R** and then continue ahead through **Kittochside**, pass drive to **Kittochside House** and you'll reach another T-junction. Cross over road here and continue along farm track ahead of you. Take 1st turning on **L** on to another farm track and, at end of this, you will be back in front of **museum** Exhibition Building.

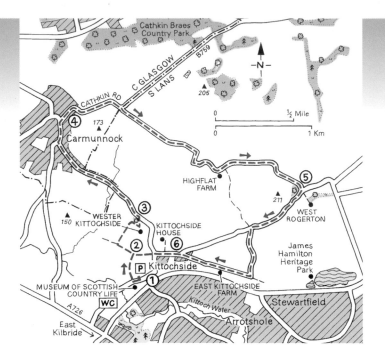

34 Whiting Bay The Spectacular Falls

2¾ miles (4.4km) 2hrs **Ascent:** 442ft (135m)

Paths: Forest paths and forest roads
Suggested map: OS Explorer 361 Isle of Arran
Grid reference: NS 047252
Parking: Car park opposite youth hostel in Whiting Bay

Enjoy this short scenic woodland walk over the Isle of Arran's ancient bedrock.

❶ From car park turn **R** on to road, cross it and turn **L** on to footpath ('Giants' Graves and Glenashdale Falls'). Follow lane until it reaches rear of house, then continue on path along river bank. Go through gate, pass forest walks sign and continue until you reach signpost pointing in direction of **Giants' Graves**.

❷ Path forks here. Go **R**, following sign to **Glenashdale Falls**. Path continues, rising gently, through wooded area, where several trees are identified by small labels fixed to trunks. Continue uphill on this path, which is marked by occasional waymarkers, crossing several bridges and fording shallow section of burn.

❸ Eventually path starts to climb steeply uphill and continues to some steps and then forks. Keep **R** and follow this path to reach falls. Keep on path past falls and continue uphill to cross bridge. The picnic table

situated on the river bank is a good spot to stop for some refreshment.

❹ From here follow path into area planted with Sitka spruce. Keep to track marked by green waymarkers as it heads through this dark part, going through gap in wall and eventually arriving at sign pointing to an Iron-Age **fort**. Turn off to look at remains of ramparts then retrace your steps to sign and continue on path.

❺ Cross bridge by another waterfall then follow more waymarkers to clearing and viewpoint – enjoy panoramic views across the glen. From here you can see the full extent of **Glenashdale Falls**. Waymarker points uphill through densely wooded area before ending at T-junction with forest road.

❻ Turn **R** on to forest road and continue, crossing water at ford and going through 3 kissing gates until route continues as metalled road. Continue along this road, go over crossroads and wind downhill. Turn **R** at T-junction and walk 200yds (183m) back to car park.

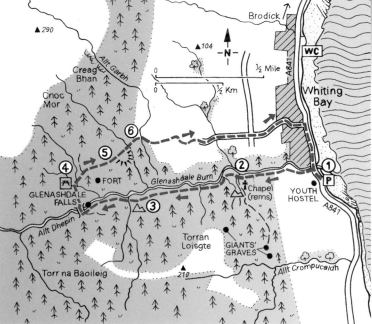

Machrie Moor Arran's Standing Stones

5½ miles (8.8km) 3hrs **Ascent:** 114ft (35m)

Paths: Footpaths, rough tracks, road, 3 stiles
Suggested map: OS Explorer 361 Isle of Arran
Grid reference: NS 898314
Parking: King's Cave car park

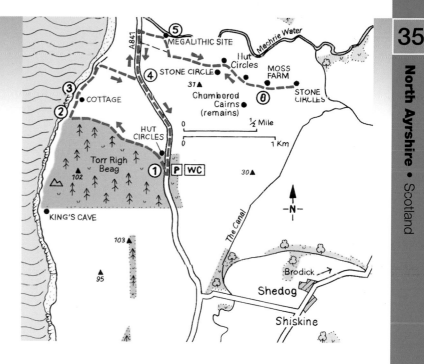

Discover the ancient standing stones of one of Scotland's finest early settlements on the Isle of Arran.

❶ From car park take footpath ('**King's Cave**'). This goes through area of woodland, past site of some **hut circles** on R and continues along edge of woods until it starts to head downhill towards sea. Look out for waymarker on R pointing back in direction you have just walked.

❷ Turn **R** here on to faint path, which in summer will be very overgrown with bracken. Plough your way through this and, in short distance, you will come to wire fence, which you can easily climb through. Cross this field and go through gate, then head downhill aiming for **L** end of white **cottage** by shore.

❸ As you near end of cottage you will see gate at corner of garden wall. Turn **R** at gate and follow line of fence on your R until you reach stile. Cross stile and turn **L** on to farm road running between 2 fences.

Keep on this road passing another cottage on R and keeping R at fork.

❹ When road ends at T-junction with **A841** turn **L**. Continue to signpost ('Machrie Moor Standing Stones'). Turn **R**, go over stile and follow access road. This rough track passes through 2 fields.

❺ In 2nd field, near far L-H corner, is a **megalithic site**, one of the oldest in the area. Nothing is to be seen above ground as the site was only identified when flints were found that were around 7,000 to 9,000 years old. Continue on road to **Moss Farm** road stone circle. Dating from approximately 2000 BC it has never been excavated.

❻ From here track continues, passing deserted **Moss Farm** then crossing stile to main stone circles of Machrie Moor. When you have finished wandering around them return to stile and take **Moss Farm** road back to **A841**. Turn **L** on to this and walk for approximately 1½ miles (2km) to return to car park.

Glasgow Alexander 'Greek' Thomson

6½ miles (10.4km) 3hrs 30min **Ascent:** 98ft (30m)

Paths: Pavements
Suggested map: OS Explorer 342 Glasgow; AA Street by Street
Grid reference: NS 587653 **Parking:** Sauchiehall Street multi-storey or on-street parking

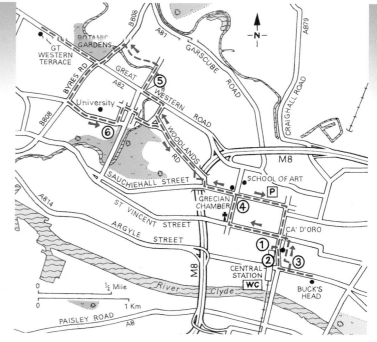

An urban walk around a Victorian city.

❶ Exit **Central Station**; turn **R**. At junction with Union Street turn **R**. The building on the opposite corner is **Ca' d'Oro**, 19th-century Italianate warehouse by John Honeyman. A little way down Union Street on the same side as Ca' d'Oro is Thomson's Egyptian Halls.

❷ Cross over then head down Union Street turning **L** into **Argyle Street** at next junction. Cross **Argyle Street**, walk along to junction with Dunlop Street to **Buck's Head** building. Cross **Argyle Street** again, retrace your steps, turning **R** into Buchanan Street. Turn **L** into Mitchell Lane, pass Lighthouse, turn **R**.

❸ Walk up Mitchell Street, continue along West Nile Street; turn **L** into **St Vincent Street**. Continue for just under ½ mile (800m), going uphill to junction with Pitt Street. You are now in front of 'Greek' Thomson's **St Vincent Street church**. Cross St Vincent Street here then head up Pitt Street to **Sauchiehall Street**.

❹ On the opposite corner is Thomson's **Grecian Chamber** (1865) and to the R along Scott Street is

Rennie Mackintosh's Glasgow **School of Art**. From front of **Grecian Chamber** turn **L**, head down **Sauchiehall Street** to Charing Cross then take pedestrian bridge over motorway to **Woodlands Road**. Go along here until it ends at Park Road, turn **R**, then **L** again into **Great Western Road**.

❺ Turn **R** into Belmont Street, **L** at Quad Gardens then **L** again at Queen Margaret Drive. Cross road and head down past **Botanic Gardens** to turn **R**, back into **Great Western Road**. Cross road and continue to Thomson's **Great Western Terrace**. Trace your steps back from here to top of **Byres Road** and turn **R** then, near bottom, turn **L** into University Avenue.

❻ Turn **L** into Oakfield Avenue, pass Eton Terrace on corner with Great George Street. Turn **R** into Great George Street, **R** at Otago Street, **L** into Gibson Street and continue when it becomes Eldon Street. Turn **R** into **Woodlands Road** and return to **Sauchiehall Street**. Follow this to junction with Renfield Street, turn **R** and head downhill to **Central Station**.

Clydeside Harbour's Tall Ship

4¾ miles (7.7km) 3hrs 30min **Ascent:** 98ft (30m) ⚠
Paths: Pavements and footpaths
Suggested map: OS Explorer 342 Glasgow; AA Street by Street
Grid reference: NS 569652 **Parking:** SECC car park beside Clyde Auditorium (Armadillo)

The last of the Clyde-built sailing ships.

❶ From Scottish Exhibition and Conference Centre (SECC) car park go on to Clyde Walkway; turn **R**, following signs to Pier 17, the **Tall Ship** and **Museum of Transport** (leave route to visit **Tall Ship**, *Glenlee*). At roundabout near **Tall Ship** on **L**, go over pedestrian bridge to cross **Clydeside Expressway**. Turn **L**; head west along pavement beside derelict building.

❷ Follow footpath when it branches **R** and goes uphill, eventually reaching junction. Go **R** under railway bridge and continue on pavement beside stone wall. Go **R** at next junction and along Old Dumbarton Road ignoring signs pointing to Kelvin Walkway. Cross road then bridge; turn **L** into Bunhouse Road.

❸ Pass **Museum of Transport** on R. At junction, cross road via pedestrian crossing and continue along lane around Kelvingrove **Museum and Art Gallery**, through car park and on to T-junction with **Kelvin Way**. Turn **L**, go over bridge and **R** through green gates on to Kelvin Walkway.

❹ Route is waymarked through **Kelvingrove Park**. Cross bridge then pass memorial to the Highland Light Infantry. Shortly after, at large bridge on **L**, path forks. Take **L** path next to river.

❺ This eventually goes uphill. Just before top of hill look for narrow path on **L** through bushes, easily missed. Go **L** here and under bridge. Turn **L** at next waymark, go over bridge and past café/bar then continue along walkway.

❻ Cross bridge, go **L** at junction, still following river. Go through tunnel and then **L** across humpback bridge to **Botanic Gardens**. Head up steps to gardens. When path reaches 3-way junction take 2nd on **R**. Pass Kibble Palace, turn **L** and follow this drive to gates and exit gardens.

❼ Cross **Great Western Road** at traffic lights and walk to end of **Byres Road**. Cross Dumbarton Road and take **R** fork. Take 2nd **L**, go along this street, cross bridge and continue past junction to end of street and under railway bridge, turning **L** to return to **SECC**.

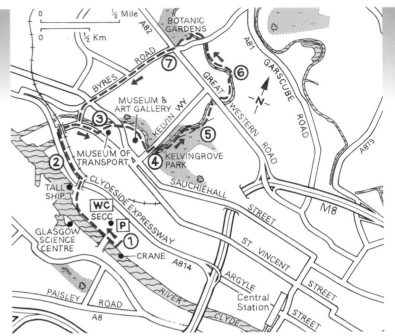

Kilsyth Along the Wall

3½ miles (5.7km) 3hrs **Ascent:** 344ft (105m) ⚠
Paths: Tow path, farm road, footpath and road
Suggested map: OS Explorer 348 Campsie Fells
Grid reference: NS 719770
Parking: Car park near old quarry at Kilsyth

Travel back in time by walking along an 18th-century canal and then a section of the Antonine's Wall.

❶ Leave car park on to main road and turn **R**. Cross over road and turn immediately **L** on to road ('Twechar and Kirkintilloch'). Continue along this road for a short while and, when it turns sharply **R**, veer off on footpath to **L** and on to tow path of the **Forth and Clyde Canal**.

❷ Go round barrier and keep on along tow path until it rejoins pavement beside main road. Take next turning on **L**, cross canal via bridge and enter **Twechar**. Continue on this road, heading uphill; near top look out for sign on **L** pointing to **Antonine Wall** and **Bar Hill**.

❸ Take next turning on **L** on to access road. Continue along here past some houses and continue on farm tracks. Go through gate and uphill. Look back the way you have come for a grand view of the canal.

❹ When you reach entrance to **Antonine Wall** go **L** through kissing gate and along lane, then through another kissing gate to access site. The wall spans Britain's narrowest land-crossing, running 40 miles (64km) from the Firth of the Forth to the Clyde. Unlike Hadrian's Wall it was built of turf, but was nonetheless substantial. Veer **L** and uphill to **Bar Hill Fort**. From top of **fort** you will see some woodland in front of you. Head for opening in trees and on to well-defined trail.

❺ Follow this trail through trees and then up on to summit of **Castle Hill**. From here, head downhill with remains of **Antonine Wall** on your L-H side. Turn **R** when your path is blocked by dry-stone wall and follow it until you intersect farm track.

❻ Turn **L** and follow this track, crossing gate, to reach T-junction with main road. Turn **L** and head downhill. Keep to **L** at roundabout, still heading downhill to reach another T-junction. From here cross road and re-enter car park.

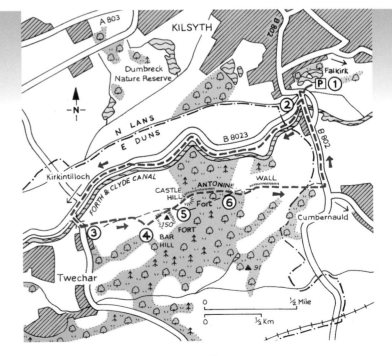

Pentland Hills Soldiers and Saints

7 miles (11.3km) 3hrs **Ascent:** 837ft (255m)
Paths: Wide firm tracks, short stretches can be muddy, 3 stiles
Suggested map: OS Explorer 344 Pentland Hills
Grid reference: NT 212679
Parking: Car park at end of Bonaly Road, by Edinburgh bypass

Across the hills near Edinburgh's reservoirs.

❶ From car park by bypass, follow signs to **Easter Kinleith** and walk along metalled track. Reach water treatment works on your L-H side. Continue past works to gate by East of Scotland Water sign.

❷ Go through kissing gate and continue, keeping **Torduff Reservoir** on L-H side. At top of **reservoir**, cross bridge and follow metalled track as it bends round to **R**. Walk under line of electricity pylons, and go over small bridge, passing artificial waterfall on L-H side, and continue past **Clubbiedean Reservoir**.

❸ Path bears **R**, with fields on both sides. Go under another line of pylons and walk to **Easter Kinleith** farm. Follow path as it bends back to **L** ('Harlaw'). Pass sign for Poets' Glen and continue over bridge and on to white house on L-H side called **Crossroads**.

❹ Turn **L** and follow sign for **Glencorse Reservoir**. Follow track, past conifer plantation on your L-H side, then cross stile next to metal gate. Continue ahead to

reach 2 more metal gates, where you cross a stile on L-H side signposted to **Glencorse**.

❺ Follow track, with hills either side; cross old stone stile. Continue in same direction to copse of conifers on R-H side, with Glencorse Reservoir ahead. Turn **L** here, following sign to Colinton by **Bonaly**.

❻ Walk uphill and maintain direction to go through gap in wire fence. Track narrows and takes you through hills, until it eventually opens out. Maintain direction to fence encircling conifers. Keep fence on L and walk down to cross stile on L-H side.

❼ Walk past **Bonaly Reservoir**, go through kissing gate and walk downhill, with good views over Edinburgh. Go through wooden gate and continue ahead, walking downhill, with trees on either side. Go through another kissing gate and follow tarmac path ahead, passing **Scout Centre** on R-H side followed by **Bonaly Tower**. Turn **L** at bridge over bypass and return to car park.

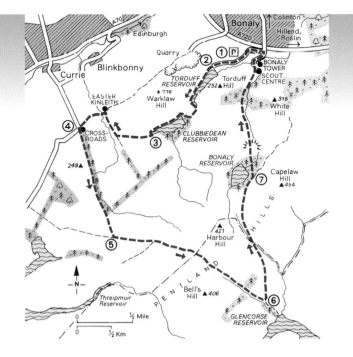

Edinburgh Old Town Murky Secrets

2 miles (3.2km) 1hr **Ascent:** 197ft (60m)
Paths: City streets, some hill tracks
Suggested map: AA Street by Street Edinburgh
Grid reference: NT 256739
Parking: Several NCP car parks in Edinburgh

Through Edinburgh's Old Town.

❶ From main entrance to **Waverley Station**, turn **L**, go to end of street, then cross and walk up Cockburn Street to **Royal Mile**. Turn **L** and walk downhill. Continue to black gates of **Holyroodhouse**. Turn **R** and walk to face new **Parliament visitor centre**.

❷ Turn **L** and follow road to **R**, then turn **R** again past **Dynamic Earth** (building looks like huge white woodlouse) and walk up into Holyrood Road. Turn **L**, walk past new buildings of *The Scotsman*, and walk up to St Mary's Street, where you turn **R** and rejoin **Royal Mile**.

❸ Turn **L**, stroll to main road, then turn **L** along South Bridge. At Chambers Street turn **R** and pass **museums**. At end of road, cross and turn **L** to see little statue of Greyfriars Bobby, a dog that refused to leave this spot after his master died.

❹ You can now cross road and make short detour into **Greyfriars Kirk** to see where Greyfriars Bobby is

buried close to his master. Or simply turn **R** and walk down Candlemaker Row. At bottom, turn **L** and wander into atmospheric **Grassmarket** – once a haunt of the body-snatchers Burke and Hare, it's now filled with shops and lively restaurants.

❺ When you've explored **Grassmarket**, walk up winding Victoria Street (it says West Bow at bottom). About two thirds of way up look out for flight of steps hidden away on **L**. Climb them and at top walk ahead to join **Royal Mile** again.

❻ Turn **L** to walk up and visit **castle**. Then walk down **Royal Mile** again, peeking into dark wynds (alleyways) that lead off it. Pass St Giles' **Cathedral** on your **R** – well worth a visit.

❼ Next on **L** pass City Chambers (under which lies the mysterious Mary King's Close). Continue to junction with Cockburn Street. Turn **L** and walk back down this winding street. At bottom, cross road and return to **Waverley Station**.

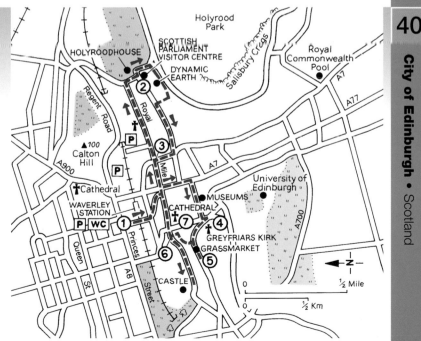

Edinburgh New Town Luring the Literati

3 miles (4.8km) 1hr 30min Ascent: 164ft (50m) 🅰

Paths: Busy city streets

Suggested map: AA Street by Street Edinburgh

Grid reference: NT 257739 **Parking:** Several large car parks in central Edinburgh

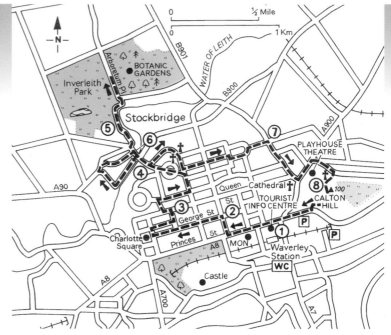

A walk in the footsteps of literary giants.

❶ From TIC, turn L and walk along **Princes Street**. Just after Scott Monument on L, cross road to Jenners department store. Continue along **Princes Street**, take R turn up Hanover Street.

❷ Take 2nd turning on L and walk along **George Street** to **Charlotte Square**. Turn R and R again to go along Young Street. At end, turn L and walk down North Castle Street to **Queen Street**.

❸ Cross road, turn L, then R down Wemyss Place and R into Heriot Row. At Howe Street turn L and, before church in middle of street, turn L and walk along South East Circus Place. Walk past Royal Circus and down into **Stockbridge**.

❹ Cross bridge, turn L along Dean Terrace. At end, turn R into Ann Street. At Dean Park Crescent turn R and follow road round into Leslie Place and into **Stockbridge** again. Cross road to walk down St Bernard's Row (almost opposite). Follow this then bear L into Arboretum Avenue.

❺ Follow road past **Water of Leith** and down to Inverleith Terrace. Cross over and walk up **Arboretum Place** to entrance to **Botanic Gardens** on R. Turn L after exploring gardens and retrace steps to **Stockbridge** again.

❻ Turn L at Hectors bar and walk uphill, then turn L along St Stephen Street. At church, follow road and turn L along Great King Street. At end, turn R, then immediately L to walk along Drummond Place, past Dublin Street and continue ahead into London Street.

❼ At roundabout turn R and walk up Broughton Street to Picardy Place. Turn L, pass statue of Sherlock Holmes, bear L towards **Playhouse Theatre**. Cross over, continue L, then turn R into Leopold Place and R again into Blenheim Place. At church turn R, walk up steps and turn L at meeting of paths.

❽ Go up steps on R, walk over **Calton Hill**, then turn R to pass cannon. Go downhill, take steps on your L and walk down into Regent Road. Turn R and walk back into **Princes Street** and start.

Leith Intoxicating Memories

3½ miles (5.7km) 1hr 30min Ascent: Negligible 🅰

Paths: Wide riverside paths and city streets

Suggested map: OS Explorer 350 Edinburgh

Grid reference: start NT 243739; finish NT 271766

Parking: Scottish National Gallery of Modern Art, Belford Road

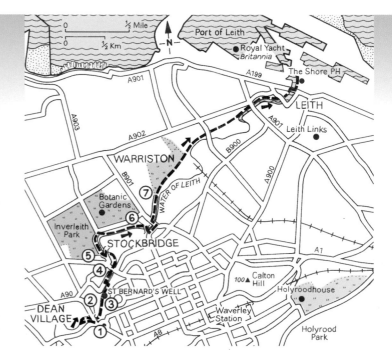

Along the river to Edinburgh's ancient port.

❶ From junction of Dean Bridge and Queensferry Street, turn L to walk down Bell's Brae. You are now in **Dean Village**, which dates back to 1128. It was once a milling centre and had 11 water mills producing meal for Edinburgh. At bottom, turn R into Miller Row.

❷ Follow this to walk under impressive arches of Dean Bridge, designed by Thomas Telford and opened in 1832. Your path then runs along bottom of steeply sided gorge, beside **Water of Leith**, and feels extremely rural. Pass old well on your L, followed by impressive **St Bernard's Well**.

❸ **St Bernard's Well** was discovered by schoolboys in 1760. The mineral water was said to have healing properties and, in 1789, the present Roman Temple was built. From here continue along main path, then go up steps. Turn L, and go R on to Dean Terrace to reach **Stockbridge**.

❹ Cross road; go down steps ahead, immediately to R of building with clock tower. Continue to follow path beside river. Where path ends, climb on to road, turn L and then R to go down Arboretum Avenue.

❺ Walk along this road, then turn R along path marked Rocheid Path. This runs beside river and is popular cycleway and jogging path. Follow this, passing backs of Colonies – low-cost housing built by Edinburgh Co-operative for artisans in the late 19th century. Walk to Tanfield Bridge.

❻ Go R, over bridge, up steps, then turn L, walking towards clock tower. At end turn L along Warriston Place, cross road. Turn R down Warriston Crescent, lined with elegant town houses. Continue to **park**.

❼ Bear R, around edge of park, then follow path uphill between trees. Turn L at top and follow cycle track ('Leith 1¼'). Follow it into **Leith**, where it brings you out near old Custom House. Bear R then L to walk along **The Shore**, before returning to town by bus.

Falkirk Reinventing the Wheel

2 miles (3.2km); 4 miles (6.4km) with monument 1hr **Ascent:** 197ft (60m)
Paths: Canal tow paths and town streets
Suggested map: OS Explorer 349 Falkirk, Cumbernauld & Livingston
Grid reference: NS 868800
Parking: Car park at Lock 10, by Union Inn

Along the canal to a 21st-century waterwheel.

❶ Start at **Union Inn** by **Lock 16**, once one of the best-known pubs in Scotland catering for canal passengers. Turn **R**, away from canal, then go **R** along road. Turn **R** along Tamfourhill Road and go through kissing gate on **L-H** side of road. (Alternatively, don't turn up Tamfourhill Road yet, but continue uphill to go under viaduct. Continue to **monument** on **L**. This commemorates the Battle of Falkirk (1298) where William Wallace was beaten by Edward I's troops.) Retrace your steps, under viaduct, turn **L** into Tamfourhill Road, and **L** through kissing gate on **L-H** side of road.

❷ This takes you on to section of Antonine Wall – there's a deep ditch and rampart behind it. Walk along parallel with Tamfourhill Road. At end go up bank on **R-H** side then down steps to join road by kissing gate.

❸ Go **L** to continue along road to another kissing gate on **L** leading you to another, shorter, section of wall. Leave wall, rejoin road and continue to mini-roundabout. Turn **L** along Maryfield Place. At end join public footpath signed to canal tow path and woodland walks. Follow this track as it winds up and over railway bridge, then on to **Union Canal**.

❹ Don't cross canal but turn **R** along tow path. This long straight stretch is popular with joggers. Eventually reach **Roughcastle tunnel** – it currently closes at 6PM to protect the Wheel from vandalism.

❺ Walk through tunnel – it's bright, clean and dry – to new **Falkirk Wheel** and another section of **Antonine Wall**. Walk on as far as **Wheel**, then continue to visitor centre at bottom. Bear **R** from here to cross bridge over **Forth and Clyde Canal**.

❻ Turn **R** and walk along tow path. Lots of dog walkers and cyclists come along here, while people frequently go canoeing along the canal. Continue to return to **Lock 16**, then turn **R** and cross canal again to return to start at **Union Inn**.

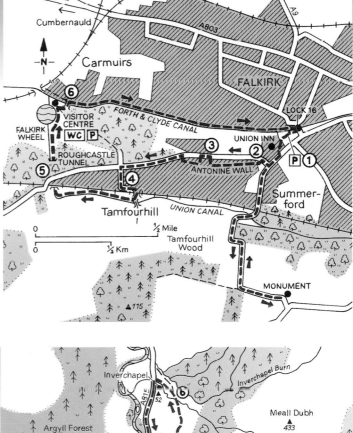

Benmore A Botanic Garden

4 miles (6.4km) 2hrs 30min **Ascent:** 459ft (140m)
Paths: Mainly forest roads and well-made footpaths, 1 stile
Suggested map: OS Explorer 363 Cowal East
Grid reference: NS 142855
Parking: Car park at Benmore Botanic Garden

Discover the story of James Duncan, the man who altered the Cowal landscape.

❶ From car park cross **A815** and follow footpath past a waymarker for Black Gates. Pass sign for Big Tree Walk and turn **R** on to surfaced lane. Continue along this lane for about 1 mile (1.6km) and just after parapet of bridge is first footpath to **Puck's Glen** on **L**.

❷ Milestone here points to Dunoon Pier 6 miles. Ignore this entrance and continue along lane until you reach car park. Turn **L** and along footpath past waymarker pole for **Puck's Glen**. Climb uphill on a steep path.

❸ At top of hill path levels out then starts to head back downhill, rather steeply on series of steps to bottom of gorge. Signpost at junction at bottom of steps points L for lower gorge and R for upper.

❹ Turn **R**, head downhill on another set of steps then cross bridge on **L** and turn **R** to head along footpath on opposite side of stream. Head uphill, cross another bridge then go past series of small waterfalls. Eventually reach yet another bridge to cross before coming to set of steps that takes you up steep part of hillside to another bridge at top. After crossing it, path levels out slightly and continues through trees to reach T-junction with forestry road.

❺ At junction there is waymarker and signpost. Turning R will lead you along forest road to Kilmun Arboretum. However, for this walk you must turn **L**, following signs for Black Gates. Because of ongoing forestry operations and renovations to several footpaths, diversions may be in place or footpaths may simply be closed.

❻ Follow signs to **L** and go on to path for Black Gates car park and, from there, return to **botanic garden**. Otherwise continue on forest road until you reach a gate near its end. Cross a stile then turn **L** at T-junction on to **A815**. Walk along here for ½ mile (800m) to return to start.

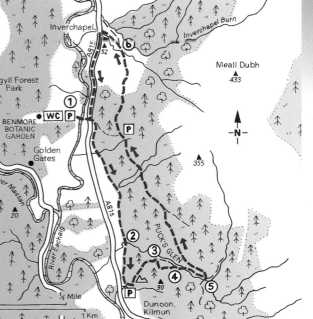

Dunardry Forest Around Mhoine Mhor

8¼ miles (13.3km) 5hrs **Ascent:** 176ft (55m) ⛰
Paths: Canal tow path, country roads and farm tracks
Suggested map: OS Explorer 358 Lochgilphead & Knapdale North
Grid reference: NR 824908
Parking: Dunardry Forest car park

A canal and Scotland's last wild peat bog.

❶ From car park descend steps, cross road and turn **L**. Continue to white cottage on **R**. Turn **R** and on to dirt track that runs behind cottage then go through gap between fence and wall. Cross canal over **Dunardry Lock** and turn **L** on to tow path.

❷ Continue to **Bellanoch** Bridge; turn **R** on to road, cross **Islandadd Bridge** and on to **B8025**. This narrow, but quiet, road is long, straight and runs through **Moine Mhor**. Continue for nearly 2 miles (3.2km); turn **R** on to unclassified road ('Drimvore').

❸ Continue for 1¾ miles (2.8km) as road runs through **National Nature Reserve** and passes farms of **Dalvore** and **Drimvore**. Finally reach T-junction with **A816** and turn **R**. After ½ mile (800m) Historic Scotland fingerpost points to **Dunadd Fort**.

❹ Turn **R** here on to long straight farm road and continue, passing farm of **Dunadd**, to Historic Scotland car park. Make your way towards hill on well-

trodden path, go past house on **L** and through kissing gate. Continue on path, following directions arrows, to emerge through gap in rocks within outer ramparts.

❺ Continue to summit and then return by same route to car park. Leave it and turn **R** on to farm track. Go through gate then, almost immediately, go **L** through 2nd and follow it as it curves **L**.

❻ Go through another just before road turns **R** and heads uphill. Continue following road going through another gate until you reach **Dunamuck** farm. Turn **L** through steading, go through gate and head downhill on farm road, continuing to T-junction with **A816**.

❼ Turn **R** on to road and follow it for ½ mile (800m) then turn **R** on to unclassified road signposted from **Cairnbaan Hotel**. After ¼ mile (400m) turn **R** on to **B841** towards Crinan. As road turns **L** across swing bridge keep straight ahead and on to canal tow path. Follow this back to **Dunardry Lock** and retrace your steps to car park.

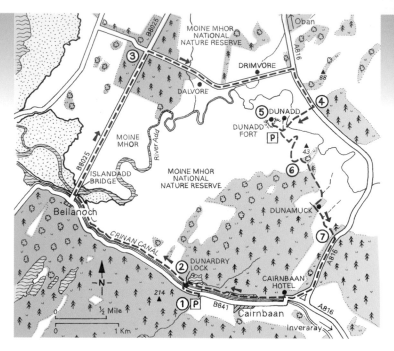

Kilmartin Glen Neolithic Monuments

3½ miles (5.7km) 3hrs **Ascent:** Negligible ⓪
Paths: Boggy fields, old coach road and country lanes, 3 stiles
Suggested map: OS Explorer 358 Lochgilphead & Knapdale North
Grid reference: NR 835988
Parking: Car park outside Kilmartin church

A short walk to the stone shrines and monuments in the valley of the ghosts.

❶ From car park visit Kilmartin church to view stones and Kilmartin Cross. Leave church, turn **L** and walk along road past **Kilmartin House**, exit village and head downhill towards garage on **L**. Just before garage turn **L**, go through kissing gate and head across field to **Glebe Cairn**.

❷ From **cairn** head half **R**, across field; cross stile. In wet weather this can be very boggy. Cross stream by bridge. Go through gate and turn **L** on to old coach road. Follow this to next **cairn**. Go **L** over a stile and follow path to visit **cairn**.

❸ Return to road and turn **L**, continuing to next **cairn**. After exploring this, follow coach road to **Kilmartin school**, where route becomes a metalled road. Go through crossroads, past **Nether Largie** farm and, ignoring **cairn** on **L**, continue short distance to **Temple Wood** ahead on **R**.

❹ Go through gate on **R** into **Temple Wood**, then return by same route. Turn **R** on to road and continue until you reach a T-junction. Turn **L** and walk along this road until you come to sign on **R** for **Ri Cruin Cairn**. Cross wall via stile and proceed along well-defined path to ancient monument.

❺ Return by same route and turn **R** on to road. Follow it to T-junction then turn **L** and keep straight ahead until you reach car park at Lady Glassary Wood. Opposite this take path to **L** ('Temple Wood'). Cross bridge, go through gate, cross another bridge and head towards **standing stones**.

❻ Turn **R** and walk across field away from **stones** towards wood. Go through gate and follow fenced path to **Nether Largie Cairn**. From here continue along fenced path, go through another gate and turn **R** on to road. Continue past **Nether Largie** farm and **Kilmartin school** and then retrace your steps back to Kilmartin church and car park.

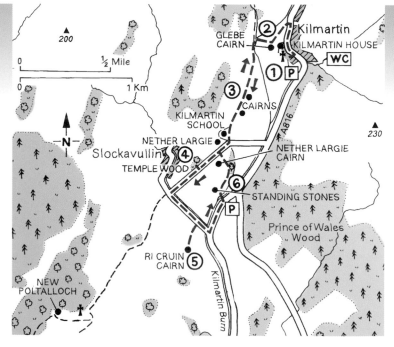

Cruachan The Hill with the Hole

2 miles (3.2km) 1hr 45min **Ascent:** 1,200ft (365m) △
Paths: Steep rugged paths, 2 ladder stiles
Suggested map: OS Explorer 377 Loch Etive & Glen Orchy
Grid reference: NN 078268
Parking: Two pull-ins on north side of A85, opposite visitor centre; lay-by ½ mile (800m) west. Not visitor centre car park

Along Loch Awe from Cruachan Reservoir.

❶ Two paths run up on either side of **Falls of Cruachan**. Both are initially rough and steep through woodland. The western one starts at tarred lane opposite entrance to **power station** (not **visitor centre**, slightly further to west). This diminishes to track, which becomes rough and crosses railway as level crossing. Path continues uphill in steep zig-zags through birch, rowan and oak. There are points to stop and look along **Loch Awe**, which disappears into distance. Path continues steeply to top of wood.

❷ Here high ladder stile crosses deer fence. With stream on your R, continue uphill on small path to track below **Cruachan dam**. Turn L, up to base of **dam**. Because it's tucked back into corrie, it can't be seen from below. Hollows between 13 huge buttresses send back echoes. Steps on L lead up below base of **dam**, then iron steps take you to top.

❸ From here look across **reservoir** and up to skyline that's slightly jagged at back L corner, where Ben Cruachan's ridge sharpens to rocky edge. In other direction, your tough ascent is rewarded by long view across low country. Turn R to **dam** end, where track leads down R to junction, then R for 50yds (46m).

❹ At this point you could stay on track to cross stream just ahead, leading to top of path used for coming up. You might wish to do this if you are concerned about ladder stile on main route. There is no clear path as you go down to L of stream, to reach this high, steep and slightly wobbly ladder stile. Below this is clear path that descends grassy slopes and gives good view of some of **Falls of Cruachan**. Inside wood, path becomes steep and rough for rest of way down. Just above railway, it turns to L, then passes under line by low tunnel beside **Falls of Cruachan Station**, to reach **A85** below.

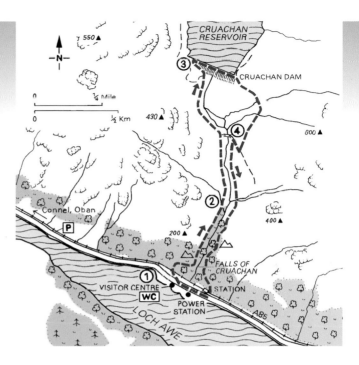

Iona Holy Island of St Columba

5¼ miles (8.4km) 3hrs 30min **Ascent:** 650ft (198m) ▲
Paths: Tracks, sandy paths, some rugged rock and heather
Suggested map: OS Explorer 373 Iona, Staffa & Ross of Mull
Grid reference: NM 286240
Parking: Ferry terminal at Fionnphort on Mull

A circuit of Iona to the marble quarry and Coracle Bay.

❶ Ferries cross to **Iona** about every hour. On island, take tarred road on **L**, passing **Martyr's Bay**. After 2nd larger bay, rejoin road as it bends **R**. Follow road across island to gate on to Iona **golf course** (please keep dogs on leads).

❷ Take sandy track ahead, then bear **L** past small cairn to shore. Turn **L** along shore to large beach. At end, bear **L** up narrow valley. After 100yds (91m) pass small concrete hut to join stony track. It passes fenced **reservoir** and drops to corner of **Loch Staoineig**. Walk along to **L** of lochan on path, improved in places, that runs gently down to **Coracle Bay**. Cross to **L** of area with furrows of lazybed cultivation – fields drained to improve crop yields – and reach shore just to **L** of rocky knoll.

❸ Route ahead is pathless and hard. If your ferry leaves in 2 hours' time or earlier, return by outward route. Otherwise, return inland for 200yds (183m) and bear **R** into little grassy valley. After 100yds (91m), go through broken wall and bear slightly **L**, past another inlet on **R**. Cross heather to eastern shoreline of island. Bear **L**, above small sea cliff, for ¼ mile (400m). Turn sharp **R** into little valley descending to remnants of **marble quarry**.

❹ Turn inland, back up valley to its head. Pass low walls of 2 ruined cottages and continue for about 200yds (183m) to fence corner. Keep fence on your L, picking way through heather, rock and bog on sheep paths. Dun I with its cairn appears ahead – aim directly for it to reach edge of fields, where fence runs across ahead. Turn R along it to small iron gate.

❺ This leads to track that passes **Ruannich** farm to tarred road of outward walk. Cross into farm track, which bends to R at **Maol**. It reaches **Baile Mor** (Iona village) at ruined **nunnery**. Just ahead is **abbey** with its squat square tower, or turn R directly to ferry pier.

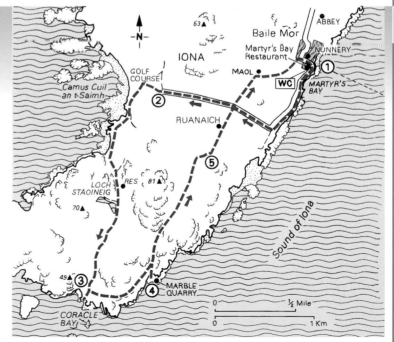

Inveraray The Castle of Cups

4 miles (6.4km) 2hrs 15min **Ascent:** 900ft (274m) ⚠️

Paths: Clear, mostly waymarked paths, no stiles
Suggested map: OS Explorer 363 Cowal East
Grid reference: NN 096085
Parking: Pay-and-display, Inveraray Pier

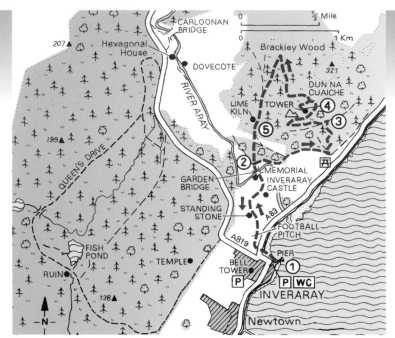

Enjoy a fine view of Inveraray.

❶ Follow seafront past Argyll Hotel and bear **L** towards **Inveraray Castle**. At 1st junction, turn **R** past **football pitch** with **standing stone**. After coach park on **L** and end wall of castle on **R**, estate road on **L** is signed 'Dun na Cuaiche Walk'. It passes a **memorial** to clansmen killed for religious reasons in 1685. Cross stone-arched **Garden Bridge** to junction.

❷ Turn **R** to riverside track and follow it to picnic table with view back to castle. Rough track runs up **L**, but turn off instead on to small path just to **R** of this, beside stone gatepost. It climbs quite steeply through area where attempts are currently being made to eradicate rhododendron.

❸ At green track above, turn **L**, slightly downhill, for 50yds (46m). Steps on **R** lead up to terraced path that goes slightly downhill around hillside for ¼ mile (400m). Turn sharp **R** up steep path with rope handrail. This works its way back around hill, passing

below small crag. Where it crosses open screes, there are fine views to R over **Inveraray**. At path junction, turn **L**, following waymarker pole up through woods. As slope eases, path crosses grassy clearing to meet wider one. Turn **L**, in zig-zags, to reach summit of **Dun na Cuaiche**. **Tower** at top is placed so it can be seen from below, but also offers outstanding views.

❹ Return down path to clearing, but this time keep ahead. Path, rather muddy, bends **L** then enters plantation and becomes clear track. It passes between 2 dry-stone pillars where wall crosses, turns back sharp **L**, and passes between 2 more pillars lower down same wall. Continue down track, ignoring sidetracks on **L**, to **lime kiln** on **R**.

❺ Below **lime kiln**, gate leads out into field. Cross it diagonally **L**, going over track to kissing gate beyond. This leads into wood of sycamores. Path runs down to track junction before **Garden Bridge** (Point ❷). Return along castle driveway to **Inveraray**.

Stirling A Braveheart

4 miles (6.4km) 2hrs **Ascent:** 279ft (85m) ⚠️

Paths: Ancient city streets and some rough tracks
Suggested map: OS Explorer 366 Stirling & Ochil Hills West
Grid reference: NS 795933
Parking: On streets near TIC or in multi-storey car parks

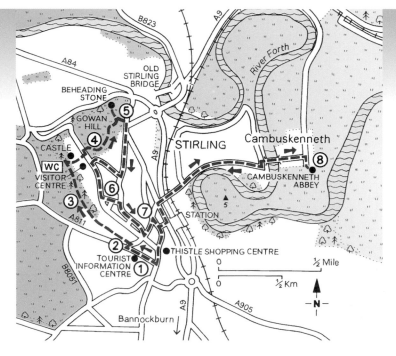

Discover the truth about William Wallace on this town trail.

❶ From **TIC** on Dumbarton Road, cross road and turn **L**. Walk past statue of Robert Burns then, just before Albert Halls, turn **R** and walk back on yourself. Just past statue of Rob Roy, turn **L** and join Back Walk.

❷ Follow path uphill, with old town wall on your **R**. Go up flight of steps that takes you on to Upper Back Wall. It's steady climb, up past Lady's Rock and on past Star Pyramid, triangular cone by graveyard.

❸ Continue following path uphill to **Stirling Castle**. Take path running downhill just to side of **visitor centre**, so **castle** is on your **L**. At bottom go **L** and walk to cemetery. Turn **R** and follow path to other side of cemetery. Bear **R** and go through gap in wall.

❹ Follow track downhill on to **Gowan Hill**. There are several branching tracks but continue on main path – heading for cannons on hill ahead. Walk down to wider grassy track, then climb uphill to **Beheading Stone**.

Retrace your steps to wide track and follow it to road.

❺ Turn **R** along Lower Bridge Street, then fork **R** into Upper Bridge Street. Continue ahead, then turn **R** down Barn Road. Follow it uphill, then go **L** at top. Eventually pass Castle Esplanade, followed by Argyll's Lodging, to reach junction.

❻ Turn **L**, passing Hermann's Restaurant and Mercat Cross. Turn **R** at bottom down Bow Street, then **L** along Baker Street. When you reach pedestrianised Friars Street, turn **L** and walk down to end.

❼ Turn **R**, then 1st **L** to **station**. Turn **L**, then **R** over bridge, continuing to riverside. Continue to join Abbey Road. Bear **L** at end, go **R** over footbridge and continue along South Street, turning **R** at end to visit remains of **Cambuskenneth Abbey**.

❽ Retrace your steps, over footbridge and back to **station**. Turn **R** at station, then **L** at top to pass **Thistle Shopping Centre**. Continue along Port Street, then turn **R** and walk along Dumbarton Road to start.

Callander Romance of Rob Roy

3 miles (4.8km) 2hrs 15min **Ascent:** 896ft (273m) ▲

Paths: Forest tracks and some rocky paths
Suggested map: OS Explorer 365 The Trossachs
Grid reference: NN 625079
Parking: Riverside car park

Steep wooded paths lead through the crags for views of the Trossachs.

❶ From car park, walk back to main road; turn **L**. Follow this, then turn **R** along Tulliepan Crescent. Just in front of new housing estate, turn **L** and follow wide track. Where track splits, take path on **L** ('The Crags').

❷ Path winds steeply uphill through trees and can get slippery after rain. Keep following path and cross footbridge. Climb to reach wall on L-H side, after which path narrows. Follow it to pass large boulder.

❸ Continue following path, which eventually bears **L**, up steps to fence. Cross footbridge, scramble over rocks and go through metal kissing gate. Eventually come to memorial **cairn**, created in 1897 for Queen Victoria's Diamond Jubilee. On a clear day there are panoramic views of the surrounding countryside.

❹ Leaving **cairn**, your path now begins to wind downhill. It is rocky in places and you'll need to take care as you descend. Eventually spot road through

trees. Turn **R** into trees and walk down to join road.

❺ Turn **R** along road – you'll see Wallace Monument in distance. Soon pass sign on R-H side for Red Well, where water runs a distinctly reddish colour owing to iron traces in the local rock. Continue to car park on your **L**. Detour here to see Bracklyn Falls.

❻ After car park, stay on road for 100yds (91m), then turn **R** to climb wooden steps – they're signposted 'The Crags Upper Wood Walk', but sign faces away from you. Walk past small building, cross little footbridge and walk to crossing of footpaths.

❼ Turn **L** for few paces, then turn **R**. Continue through woods, cross footbridge and at wider, slate-covered track, turn **R** uphill. At end of track, turn **L** and walk downhill to wooden seat and footbridge.

❽ Take path that runs to **R** of seat (don't cross footbridge). Follow path downhill back to place where you entered woods. Turn **R**, then go **L** along main road back into **Callander** to car park.

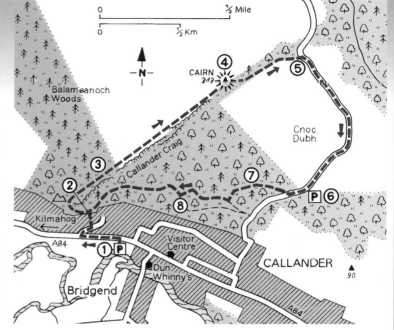

The Whangie A Gash in the Rock

2½ miles (4km) 3hrs **Ascent:** 515ft (157m) ▲

Paths: Hill tracks and well-trodden footpaths, 2 stiles
Suggested map: OS Explorer 347 Loch Lomond South
Grid reference: NS 511808
Parking: Queen's View car park

The hidden training ground of generations of rock climbers.

❶ Head toward **L** of car park on to small hillock where Queen Victoria stood for her first view of Loch Lomond. Descend and cross stile over wall where well-defined path crosses duckboards and meanders uphill. Turn **R** to follow edge of wood. After duckboards this is pleasant grassy walk.

❷ As you get to top, near fence, admire view. Look away to your **R** for expanse of Loch Lomond and Ben Lomond towering over it to R and Arrochar Hills away to L. Cross ladder stile over fence; turn **R** on to narrow but well-trodden path. Follow this along side of hill.

❸ When path forks go **L** and head uphill. As you near top you will see Ordnance Survey pillar on summit of **Auchineden Hill**. Head towards this by any route you find. Ground round here is often boggy and several attempts may be required to find best way across it. To the south from here are the Kilpatrick Hills and, beyond

them, the River Clyde. Look for Burncrooks Reservoir to your **R** and Kilmannan Reservoir to your **L**. Beyond is Cochno Loch, another reservoir and popular excursion for Clydebank residents.

❹ Looking towards Ben Lomond, the area in front of you is Stockie Muir. Walk towards Ben on path leading away from OS pillar and go downhill into dip. Another path runs across this. Turn **L** on to it and follow it round side of small hill. Where path curves **R** look for crags on R.

❺ Here you'll find hidden opening to **The Whangie**. It's easy to miss so look out for spot on **R** for easy climb few steps up to crags and it's as if wall opens up in front of you. Climb into **The Whangie** and walk to other end on path.

❻ Exit **The Whangie** and head to **R** on another footpath. Continue on this until it rejoins path you took on uphill journey. Go back to stile then retrace your steps downhill and back to car park.

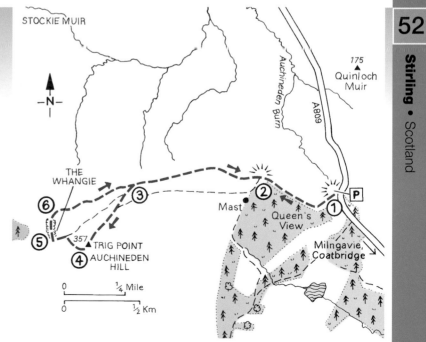

53 Aberfoyle Queen Elizabeth Forest Park

4 miles (6.4km) 3hrs Ascent: 446ft (136m) 🔺3

Paths: Forest roads and footpaths
Suggested map: OS Explorer 365 The Trossachs
Grid reference: NN 519014
Parking: At visitor centre near Aberfoyle

The Highland Boundary Fault and along a 19th-century inclined railway.

① From front of **visitor centre** turn **L**, go down steps on to footpath and follow blue waymarkers of **Highland Boundary Fault Trail**. Continue on this trail to reach **Waterfall** of the Little Fawn with its 55ft (16.7m) drop. Shortly after this turn **L** to cross bridge then **R** following white arrow **L** again on to forest road.

② This is part of **National Cycle Route (NCN)** so look out for cyclists. Head uphill on this road following blue **Highland Boundary Fault** markers and **NCN** Route 7 signs. When road forks at junction, keep **L** continuing uphill until you reach crossroads.

③ Turn **R**, at blue waymarker, on to smaller, rougher road. **Boundary Fault Trail** parts company with NCN Route 7 here. The going is easy along here. Continue until you eventually reach viewpoint and seat on **R**.

④ From here. road heads uphill until it reaches waymarker near path heading uphill towards **mast**.

Turn **R** then go through barrier and start descending. Although this is well-made path it is nevertheless very steep descent through woods and great care should be taken.

⑤ This path follows line of **Limecraigs Railway** an early 19th-century inclined railway used for transporting limestone. It continues downhill to go through another barrier where path is intersected by forest road. Cross this road, go through another barrier and once again head downhill.

⑥ At bottom of hill is set of steps leading to forest road. Turn **R** on to road and follow blue waymarkers. Stay on this road until you reach green signpost on **L** pointing to **visitor centre**. Turn **L** on to downhill track and head through woods.

⑦ Eventually you will reach board announcing end of trail. From here route is signed back to **visitor centre**. When trail forks take **R-H** turning and head uphill beside handrail and return to start.

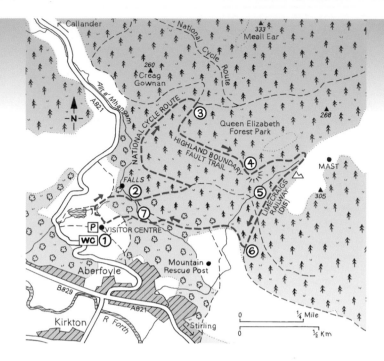

54 Aberfoyle Great Forest of Loch Ard

3½ miles (5.7km) 2hrs Ascent: 98ft (30m) 🔺1

Paths: Roads, forest roads and trails
Suggested map: OS Explorer 365 The Trossachs
Grid reference: NS 521009
Parking: Car park at Aberfoyle beside tourist office in centre of town

Discover the Stone of Destiny's hiding place and birthplace of the Scottish Parliament.

① Leave from west end of car park and turn **L** into Manse Road. Cross narrow bridge over **River Forth** (river has its source near here although it is more usually associated with Edinburgh) and continue along grass beside road until 1st junction on R. Turn **R** here and head uphill, passing **Covenanters Inn**. Short distance past here is open countryside and start of **Great Forest of Loch Ard**.

② Head straight on along forest road, keeping an ear open for heavy timber lorries. During week this can get fairly busy, as this is main forestry extraction route, so keep well into side. After approximately ½ mile (800m) you will reach staggered crossroads. Continue straight ahead along forest road until you come to turning on R with yellow waymarker. Turn **R** here.

③ Follow waymarked trail through forest almost to banks of **Duchray Water**. This rises on the north face

of Ben Lomond and joins with **Avondhu** from **Loch Ard** to create the **River Forth** near **Aberfoyle**. Path curves **R**, continues to descend slightly to junction.

④ Turn **R** and follow path through trees to north banks of **Lochan Spling**. Path then swings **L** and, at end of **Lochan**, turns **R** at waymarker pole, crosses small stream and heads slightly uphill.

⑤ When path reaches T-junction, turn **L** and rejoin main forest access road continuing along it to **Covenanters Inn**. This takes its name not from the activities of the 17th-century Scottish Presbyterians, who were persecuted by the Stuartt monarchy for refusing to give up their faith, but to the activities of 20th-century Scottish Nationalists.

⑥ Continue past **inn**, where later a group of Nationalists temporarily hid Scotland's Stone of Destiny when it was liberated from Westminster Abbey in 1950, then turn **L** on to Manse Road at junction and return to start.

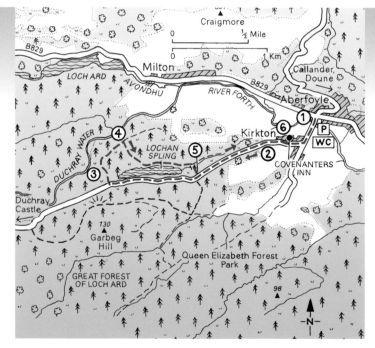

Loch Lomond The Sallochy Woods

2 miles (3.2km) 2hrs 30min **Ascent:** 131ft (40m)
Paths: West Highland Way, forest trail and forest road
Suggested map: OS Explorer 364 Loch Lomond North
Grid reference: NS 380957
Parking: Sallochy Woods car park

A gentle stroll by the bonnie banks of Loch Lomond, Britain's largest fresh water lake.

1 From car park head towards entrance on to main road. Go **R** on to track beside starting post to **Sallochy Trail**. Cross over road with care and then continue along trail on other side. This trail runs alongside some woodland which you should keep on your R-H side. Continue and, when path eventually forks, keep **R** and go into wood following obvious waymarker posts. The diverse woods here are part of the **Queen Elizabeth Forest Park** and contain a staggering variety of animals and plants. Over a quarter of the plants that flourish in Britain can be found here. You may spot a rare capercaillie (It's the size of a turkey), ptarmigan or even a golden eagle.

2 Trail goes through wood and then passes into ruined 19th-century farm steading of **Wester Sallochy**, which Forestry Commission has now cleared of trees. Several buildings can be seen and it

is worth spending some time investigating these old ruins. When you have finished, circle buildings to **L** and follow well-worn trail until it ends at T-junction beside waymarker post. Turn **R** on to forest road here.

3 Follow forest road for about ½ mile (800m) to reach gate just before junction with main road. Cross gate, then cross main road and turn **R**. Look carefully for faint track running through woods to your **L**.

4 Follow faint track back towards **loch** (if you miss track then enter wood at any point and head west towards **loch**). When track intersects with well-surfaced footpath turn **R** on to **West Highland Way**. Follow waymarkers, keeping on main path and ignoring any subsidiary tracks branching off it.

5 Follow path uphill through rocky section and then, as it levels off, through wood. There is some boggy ground here but strategically placed duckboards make going easier. Eventually trail passes through **Sallochy Woods** car park returning you to start.

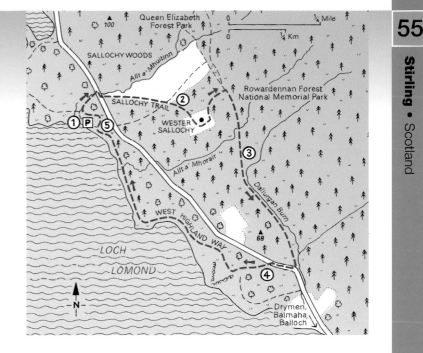

Balquhidder On the Trail of an Outlaw

2½ miles (4km) 2hrs **Ascent:** 328ft (100m)
Paths: Forest roads and hillside, 2 stiles
Suggested map: OS Explorer 365 The Trossachs
Grid reference: NN 536209
Parking: At Balquhidder church

On the trail of the Highland outlaw, Rob Roy, and on to see his final resting place.

1 From car park at **Balquhidder church**, walk along dirt track, go past shed and cross stile on **R** side which gives access to forest. Follow direction arrows on green signposts pointing to **Creag an Tuirc** along forest track and heading up hill.

2 Continue on this obvious trail for about ½ mile (800m) then turn **R**, beside green building, again following clearly signposted route along forest road. After another ½ mile (800m) cross gate on R-H side, go slightly downhill on some stone steps and across small stream.

3 Path now heads uphill on some stone steps, through old pine trees and on towards summit of knoll. Here is cairn erected by Clan Maclaren Society in 1987 to commemorate their 25th anniversary. The plaque proclaims that this place is the ancient rallying point of their clan.

4 A seat below the cairn is a grand place to rest after the climb up here. Sit for a while and enjoy superb views over the meandering line of **River Balvag** and the length of **Loch Voil** with Braes of Balquhidder rising steeply above it. You can see the route that Rob Roy's funeral procession would have taken from Inverlochlarig down to the village itself, and the churchyard where his body lies. Now retrace your steps back down hill but before reaching top of stone steps which you came up, take path to **L** ('Forest Walk'). This continues downhill following waymarked poles, down some steps and across small bridge. Path goes through bracken, over small stream and across stile. Eventually it will pass through small wood of young native trees before emerging on to forest road.

5 Turn **L** here and retrace your steps back downhill over stile and turn **L** to return to car park. From here enter churchyard and turn **L**. **Rob Roy's grave** is on **L** in front of ruins of pre-Reformation church.

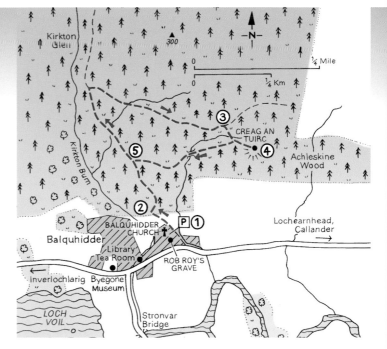

57 Loch Katrine Along the Shore

6¾ miles (10.9km) 4hrs 30min **Ascent:** 420ft (128m) ⚠

Paths: Waterboard roads, hill tracks
Suggested map: OS Explorers 364 Loch Lomond North; 365 The Trossachs
Grid reference: NN 404102 (on Explorer 364)
Parking: Car park at Stronachlachar Pier

A walk around Glasgow's water supply in the heart of the Trossachs.

❶ From car park follow road back towards **B829** and take 2nd turning on **L**. This is access road for Scottish Water vehicles only. Continue along access road until you come to cattle grid with green gateposts at building known as **Royal Cottage**. Turn **R** just before this on to rough gravel track that heads through some dense bracken.

❷ As path emerges on to open hillside you will see 1st of several ventilation shafts and beyond it, on hill, strange **obelisk.** Follow path along this line. When you reach the **obelisk** be sure to look back for super views over **Loch Katrine** below and across to the hills with their narrow passes where Rob Roy and his men moved from **Loch Katrine** to Balquhidder and beyond, moving cattle or escaping from forces of law and order. Continue following line of ventilation shafts towards chimney-like structure on top of hill. From

here go **R** and downhill. Take great care on this section as path has eroded and is very steep. At bottom, go through gap at junction of two fences. From here go **L.**

❸ Follow well-defined track that goes through some pine trees and past another ventilation **shaft.** Keep **L** at **shaft.** It can be very muddy on this short stretch. Continue on path until it intersects forest road by stream. Cross road and look for faint track continuing downhill in same direction. In summer this path may be difficult to find because it's hidden by bracken. In this case follow line of telephone poles. Eventually after working downhill through more woodland track emerges on to **B829.**

❹ Turn **R** here and follow road. It will eventually emerge from **Loch Ard Forest** into open countryside. **Loch Arklet** can be seen on **L**; it is now connected to **Loch Katrine** by underground pipeline. When road reaches T-junction with Inversnaid road, turn **R**. When road forks, turn **R** and return to **Stronachlachar Pier.**

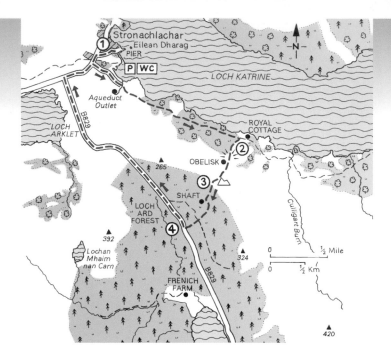

58 Carbeth The Hut Community

3 miles (4.8km) 2hrs 30min **Ascent:** 98ft (30m) ⚠

Paths: Roads, access tracks and footpaths, 1 stile
Suggested map: OS Explorer 348 Campsie Fells
Grid reference: NX 524791
Parking: Carbeth Inn, check beforehand with landlord

Discover a working class Utopian dream.

❶ From car park at **Carbeth Inn** turn **R** on to A809. After ¼ mile (400m) take 1st turning **R** on to **B821**. Continue on this road for 1 mile (1.6km) passing huts on **L** and ignoring public footpath sign to **R**.

❷ Turn **R** at signpost for **West Highland Way**. There's also Scottish Rights of Way Society signpost beside this pointing to Khyber Pass Road to Mugdock Country Park – the favoured route of early walkers heading out of Glasgow to the Campsie Fells.

❸ Go through gate and continue along well-surfaced access road. Ignoring Kyber Pass turn-off, keep **R** and go over stile to follow **West Highland Way** along access road to more huts. After passing some huts on **R** and another hut on **L** look out for partially concealed public path signpost on **R** beside **West Highland Way** marker post.

❹ Turn **R** here on to narrow but well-surfaced footpath and continue along it, passing **Carbeth Loch**

on R-H side, to reach junction with drive leading to **Carbeth House.** This is a private house and is not open to the public. Turn **L**, pass house on **R** then take next turning on **L.**

❺ Continue along this lane ignoring public right of way sign pointing **R**, then head uphill to reach another grouping of **Carbeth huts.** At 1st hut, green one, road forks with narrow path branching to **R**. Ignore this and take wider road which passes to **L** of hut.

❻ Keep on this road as it passes through main part of **Carbeth huts**, extraordinary assortment of small dwellings, shanties and shacks. Ignore all smaller tracks branching off this road; they allow access to individual huts or other parts of the settlement.

❼ Eventually pass much larger hut on **R**, then smaller green one with fenced garden on **L**, and follow road as it curves to **L**. Continue downhill on this to reach T-junction with **A809** beside **Carbeth Inn.** Turn **R** and return to car park.

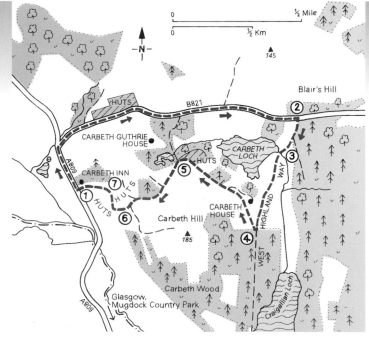

Culross A Leisurely Circuit

3 miles (4.8km) 1hr 30min **Ascent:** 180ft (55m)
Paths: Generally firm paths, some muddy woodland tracks
Suggested map: OS Explorer 367 Dunfermline & Kirkcaldy
Grid reference: NS 983859 **Parking:** Culross West car park

An easy walk around an historic town.

❶ Turn **L** out of car park and walk along road, with bay to **L** and housing to **R**. Continue, past cottages, to edge of town. Take care of traffic now as there is no pavement. Pass entrance to **Dunimarle Castle** on **R** and continue to entrance to **Blair Castle** – now a memorial home for miners.

❷ Turn **R** and walk up tarmac drive ('private') which is lined with rhododendrons. Walk until you see **castle** on **L**. Before you reach it, take **R-H** turning in trees and follow it as it bears **R**. Continue to **Blair Mains** farmhouse on **L**.

❸ Continue on track, walking under line of pylons with fields on either side. Walk ahead towards trees and continue to gate on **L-H** side. Look carefully to spot wooden fence post on **R-H** side, with words 'West Kirk' and 'grave' painted on it in white. Take narrow **R-H** path immediately before it, through trees.

❹ Follow this path and then go through kissing gate and continue ahead, with trees on your **L** and fields on your **R**. Go through another kissing gate, and continue as path opens out to wider, grassy track. At crossing of paths, continue ahead along narrow path and walk under a line of pylons. Soon pass remains of **church** on **L-H** side.

❺ Continue ahead, past old cemetery, until track joins tarmac road. Walk in same direction to junction. Turn **R** and then head downhill – watch out for traffic now as road can be busy. Soon reach **Culross Abbey** on **L-H** side.

❻ Stop to visit **abbey**. Continue to walk on downhill, down Tanhouse Brae, to soon reach Mercat (old Market) Cross, with **The Study** on **R-H** side. Continue in same direction, down Back Causeway, to reach main road.

❼ Turn **R**, walk past tourist information centre, past Tron (old burgh weighing machine), then past large ochre-coloured building on **R**, **Culross Palace**. To reach starting point, continue in same direction – car park is on **L-H** side, just past children's play area.

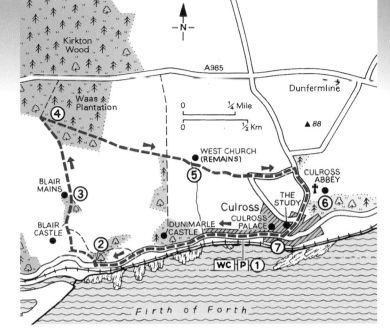

St Andrews Academic Traditions

4½ miles (7.2km) 2hrs **Ascent:** 33ft (10m)
Paths: Ancient streets and golden sands
Suggested map: OS Explorer 371 St Andrews & East Fife
Grid reference: NO 506170
Parking: Free parking along The Scores, otherwise several car parks

A town trail to an ancient university.

❶ With Martyrs **Monument** on The Scores in front of you, walk **L** past bandstand. At road turn **R**, walk to British Golf **Museum**, then turn **L**. Pass clubhouse of **Royal and Ancient Golf Club** on your **L**, then bear **R** at burn to reach beach.

❷ Your route now takes you along **West Sands**. Walk as far as you choose, then either retrace your steps along beach or take any path through dunes to join tarmac road. Walk back to Golf **Museum**, then turn **R** and walk to main road.

❸ Turn **L** and walk to St Salvator's College. Peek through archway at serene quadrangle – and look at initials PH in cobbles outside. They commemorate Patrick Hamilton, who was martyred here in 1528 – they say students who tread on the site will fail their exams. Cross over and walk to end of College Street.

❹ Turn **R** and walk along Market Street. At corner turn **L** along Bell Street, then **L** again on South Street.

Just after you pass Church Street, cross over into quadrangle of St Mary's College. Join path on **R** and walk up to reach Queen's Terrace.

❺ Turn **R** to reach red-brick house, then **L** down steeply sloping Dempster Terrace. At end cross burn, turn **L** and walk to main road. Cross and walk along Glebe Road. At park, take path that bears **L**, walk past play area and up to Woodburn Terrace.

❻ Turn **L** to join St Mary Street, turn **L** again, then go **R** along Woodburn Place. Bear **L** beside beach. You'll get good views of **Long Pier**, where students traditionally walked on Sunday mornings. Cross footbridge and join road.

❼ Bear **R** for few paces, then ascend steps on **L** to remains of church and on to famous ruined **cathedral**. Gate in wall on **L** gives access to site.

❽ Your route then takes you past ancient **castle** on **R**, former palace/fortress. Pass Castle Visitor Centre, then continue along The Scores to return to start.

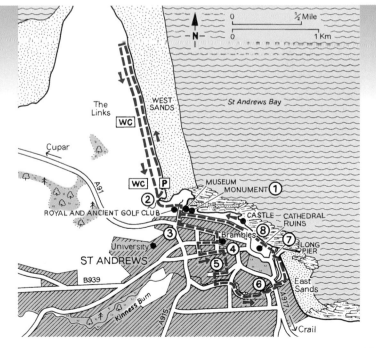

61 East Neuk A Fishy Trail

4 miles (6.4km) 1hr 30min **Ascent:** 49ft (15m) ⚠
Paths: Well-marked coastal path, 3 stiles
Suggested map: OS Explorer 371 St Andrews & East Fife
Grid reference: start NO 613077; finish NO 569034
Parking: On street in Crail

A linear coastal walk through East Neuk.

❶ From **tourist information centre** in Crail, walk down Tolbooth Wynd. At end turn **R**, continue to garage, bear **L** ('no vehicular access to harbour'). Walk by old castle wall to lookout point and view of harbour. Bear **R** to High Street.

❷ Turn **L** along road, passing 2 white beacons, which help guide boats into harbour. Turn **L**, walk down West Braes ('Coast Path'). At Osbourne Terrace bear slightly **L**, go down steps, through kissing gate and on to grassy track by shore.

❸ Follow path as it hugs shoreline. Soon see cormorants on rocks to your **L** and views of Isle of May. Go down steps, over slightly boggy area and continue to reach 2 derelict cottages – area known as **The Pans**.

❹ Pass cottages and continue along shore, cross stone stile. Pass flat rocks on **L** covered with interesting little rock pools. Cross burn by footbridge –

see Bass Rock and Berwick Law on your **L** and village of **Anstruther** ahead. Soon reach **caves**.

❺ Pass **caves**, cross stone stile on **L-H** side and then footbridge. Track is narrower now and passes fields **R**, then maritime grasses **L**. Big stepping stones take you to another stile; cross them to reach **Caiplie**.

❻ Go through kissing gate by houses, follow wide grassy track, go through kissing gate to walk past field. Path now runs past free-range pig farm and up to **caravan park**.

❼ Continue along shore, following track to play area and war memorial on **R**. Continue to enter Cellardyke and on to harbour. Pass it and **The Haven** restaurant; continue on John Street then on James Street.

❽ At end of James Street maintain direction, then follow road as it bends down to **L**. Walk past guiding beacon and into **Anstruther's** busy little harbour. You can now either walk back to **Crail** or take bus which leaves from harbour.

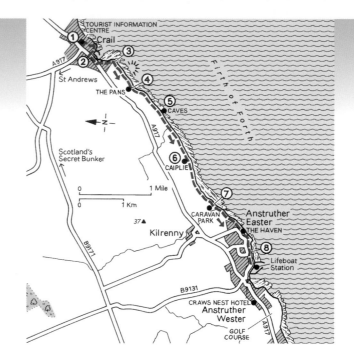

62 Perth Along the Tay to Scone

4 miles (6.4km) 1hr 30min **Ascent:** Negligible ⚠
Paths: City streets and wide firm tracks
Suggested map: OS Explorer 369 Perth & Kinross
Grid reference: NO 114237
Parking: On street in Perth

A town trail around Perth with views over Scotland's ancient capital.

❶ From **TIC** turn **R**, then take 1st **R** and walk around building. Turn **R** again and walk down to road. Cross and take **R-H** road ahead, passing bus stops. Walk down to Kinnoul Street, then cross and join Mill Street.

❷ Continue down Mill Street, passing Perth **Theatre** on R-H side. Pass **Caffe Canto** on R-H side, and join Bridge Lane. Pass **museum and art gallery** on L-H side and reach Charlotte Street. Turn **L**.

❸ At corner turn **L** to visit Fair Maid's House. Otherwise, cross road and turn **R** through park. Pass war memorial then bear **L** to join riverside path and good views of smart houses along opposite bank.

❹ Continue ahead, passing **golf course**. At sign for 14th tee, turn **R** and follow track. At end there's wall on **L**. Here either go **L** of wall along enclosed cycle track (keeping ear open for cyclists), or go **R** of it to walk by water's edge.

❺ Follow your chosen track until 2 tracks meet, just past electricity sub station. Walk by riverside now to enjoy great views of **Scone Palace** on opposite bank – there's a seat for a break.

❻ Retrace your steps, walking back beside river or along cycle track and back to **golf course**. Turn **L** and walk back towards **Perth** until you reach cricket and football pitches on R-H side.

❼ Turn **R** and walk between pitches to join Rose Terrace – John Ruskin once lived here. Turn **L**, then bear **L** at end into Charlotte Street and **R** into Bridge Lane again. Turn **L** along Skinner Gate, site of the oldest pub in Perth, and walk to end.

❽ Cross over to pass **St John's Kirk**. Cross South Street and join Princes Street. At Marshall Place turn **L** and walk to **Fergusson Gallery** on L-H side. Then turn back along Marshall Place, walk up to King Street, then turn **R**. Maintain direction, then turn **L** into West Mill Street and return to start of walk.

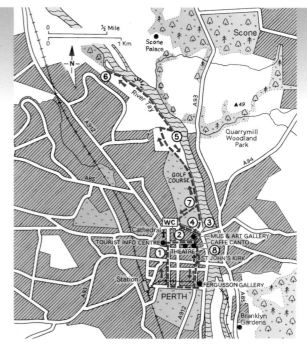

Fortingall An Ancient Yew

3½ miles (5.6km) 2hrs **Ascent:** 33ft (10m)

Paths:	Quiet roads and firm farm tracks, 1 stile
Suggested map:	OS Explorer 378 Ben Lawers & Glen Lyon
Grid reference:	NN 741470
Parking:	Fortingall village

An easy walk amidst mountain scenery.

1 With your back to **Fortingall Hotel**, turn **R** along road, passing several pretty thatched cottages (unusual in Scotland) on R-H side. Follow road over burn and past entrance to Glen Lyon farm. Eventually reach fork in road.

2 Ignore R-H fork and keep ahead. Road soon crosses bridge over **River Lyon**.

3 Just over bridge turn **R** and follow road (it's tarmacked but very quiet), and walk past some little cottages on R-H side. Continue ahead until you reach sign for Duneaves.

4 Turn **L** and follow road – river is on your L-H side. You feel as if you're in a secret valley as you walk along here, and in late summer you can stop to pick wild raspberries that grow by the roadside. Continue past area of woodland, after which you get views across valley to **Fortingall**.

5 Continue to follow road until you see white house on R-H side. Leave metalled track and turn **L** at pylon just before house – good views of surrounding hills.

6 Follow wide, stony track as it leads down to **Duneaves**. Just before you reach house go through rusty gate in wall on R-H side. Then walk across field, maintaining your direction to go over rather bouncy footbridge. Bear **R** after crossing bridge, then go through gate and join road.

7 Turn **L** and walk back along road. Soon pass 2 sets of **standing stones** in field on **L** – 6 stones in a ring near the road, and 3 further away. Walk back into **Fortingall** to reach the starting point. Note the ancient tree in the churchyard at Fortingall. It is generally reckoned to be about 5,000 years old and is the oldest living thing in Europe, and possibly the world. In 1769 the tree's girth was measured and was found to be 56ft (17m).

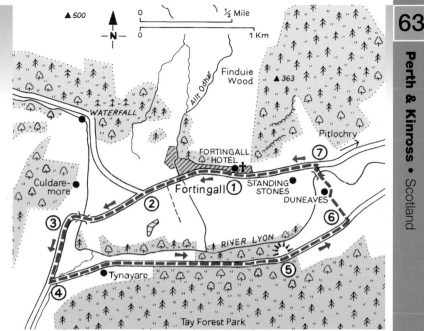

Alyth The Sweet Fruits

5 miles (8km) 3hrs **Ascent:** 787ft (240m)

Paths:	Wide grassy tracks, some rougher paths on hill
Suggested map:	OS Explorer 381 Blairgowrie, Kirriemuir & Glamis
Grid reference:	NO 236486
Parking:	Car park in Alyth Market Square

Through the fertile heart of Scotland.

1 From Market Square, cross burn, then turn **L** along Commercial Street, so river is on your L-H side. Turn **R** up Tootie Street, **R** again up Hill Street, then take Loyal Road on **L**. Continue uphill to reach sign ('Hill of Loyal Walk').

2 Walk uphill now, go through gate and continue in same direction, walking past wood on R-H side. Go through kissing gate, passing area that in summer is mass of purple foxgloves. Eventually path levels out and then starts to bear downhill. Maintain direction to go through kissing gate and over burn.

3 Here path becomes narrower and bears uphill, becoming muddier and more overgrown. Walk under trees, through gate and leave birch and oak woodland. Keep an eye out for deer here, as I spotted one bounding into the trees, just a few feet away from me. Maintain direction through grass, then go through kissing gate to road.

4 Turn **L**; walk along generally quiet road ('**Hill of Alyth Walk**'). Pass conifer plantation, house on R-H side and go over cattle grid. Soon turn **L** and follow signs ('Cateran Trail').

5 Walk uphill and, at crossing of tracks, turn to **R**. When ground flattens, turn **L** uphill. At another crossing of paths, turn **R**. There are lots of paths traversing hill, so choose your own route here, but essentially you must keep lakes on your **L** and don't walk as far as beacon. Make for small copse on your **R**, between 2 farmhouses, then go through gate.

6 Walk downhill along enclosed track – you'll see the spire of the church below. When you reach another track turn **L** and then **R** to continue downhill on metalled track. Walk under line of pylons and come into village by church.

7 Path now bears **L** and downhill, past phone box on L-H side. Turn **R**, walking past crumbling old arches, and retrace your steps to Market Square.

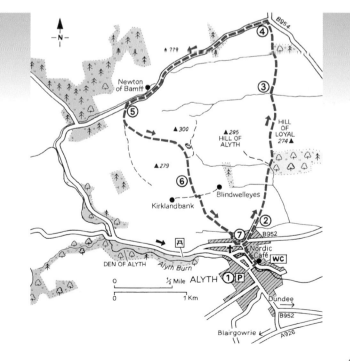

65 Loch Rannoch The Black Wood

3¾ miles (6km) 2hrs 30min **Ascent:** 1,150ft (350m)

Paths: Forest roads, rough woodland paths, no stiles

Suggested map: OS Explorer 385 Rannoch Moor & Ben Alder

Grid reference: NN 590567

Parking: Small pull-in just west of Rannoch School

In the ancient Caledonian forest.

1 From pull-in, walk back along road with **Loch Rannoch** on your L and **Rannoch School** on R. Pass commando climbing tower on R, **sailing centre** on L and **golf course**. At **school's** goods entrance, Scottish Rights of Way Society (SRWS) signpost points up to R – this is old and unused through route to Glen Lyon. Follow tarred driveway past tennis courts to 1st buildings and turn **L** at another SRWS signpost.

2 Sketchy path runs up under birch trees. At empty gateway in rotting fence it enters larch trees and becomes narrow track that's slightly damp in places. Avoid lesser path turning off to L; main one becomes green path contouring across slope with glimpses of **Loch Rannoch** on R. Path runs up to wide forest road.

3 Ignore path continuing opposite and turn **R**, contouring around hill. Clear-felling has opened up views to **Loch Rannoch** and the remote hills beyond. The highest of these, with a steep right edge, is Ben Alder, the centre of the southern Highlands. This hill is glimpsed from many places but isn't easily reached from anywhere. After ½ mile (800m), keep ahead where another track joins from L. Joined tracks descend to triangle junction. Turn **L**, gently uphill and, after 220yds (201m), bear **R** on to little-used old track. This descends to bridge over **Dall Burn**.

4 Some 120yds (110m) after bridge, track bends **L** and here path descends on **R**. This is the **Black Wood of Rannoch**, now a forest reserve. Path runs under beautiful pines and birches. On **R**, **Dall Burn** is sometimes in your sight and can always be heard. Path is quite rough, but unmistakable as it cuts through deep bilberry and heather. After 1 mile (1.6km), path bends **L** to track. Turn **R** to leave Caledonian Reserve at notice board. At T-junction, turn **L**, away from bridge leading into **Rannoch School**. Track improves as it runs past school's indoor **swimming pool** to lochside road.

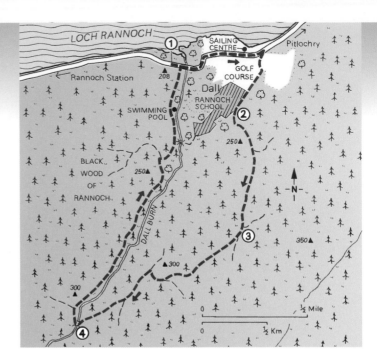

66 Glen Tilt A Royal Route

6½ miles (10.4km) 3hrs 15min **Ascent:** 852ft (250m)

Paths: Estate tracks and smooth paths, 1 stile. Note: Track through firing range is closed a few days each year (mostly weekdays). Consult Atholl Estate Ranger service

Suggested map: OS Explorers 386 Pitlochry & Loch Tummel; 394 Atholl

Grid reference: NN 866662 (on Explorer 386) **Parking:** Castle main car park

Following Queen Victoria's route through the Grampians.

1 Turn **R** in front of **castle** to 4-way signpost, bear **R** for gate into Diana's Grove. Bear **L** on wide path to **Diana** herself. Turn **R** on path to giant redwood, bear **L** to cross **Banvie Burn** on footbridge alongside road bridge. Gate leads to road.

2 Now at **Old Blair**, turn **R** and follow Minigaig Street uphill. It eventually becomes track and enters forest. Ignore track on L and, in ¼ mile (400m), fork **R**. In 60yds (55m) pass path down to R with green waymarker. This is return route if **firing range** ahead is closed. Otherwise keep ahead to emerge from trees at **firing range** gate.

3 Red flag flies here if **range** is in use, but read notice as on most firing days track route through **range** may be used. Follow main track downhill, below **firing range** targets, to riverside, then fork **R** to **Gilbert's Bridge**.

4 Cross and turn **R** over cattle grid. Follow track for 220yds (201m). Turn **L** up steep path under trees to stile. Green track now runs down-valley. Once through gate into wood, keep on main track, uphill. After the gate out of the wood, there's a view to Schiehallion. Another gate leads on to gravel track then tarred road.

5 Turn **R**, down long hill, crossing **waterfalls** on way down. At foot of hill turn **R** ('**Old Blair**'), to cross **Old Bridge of Tilt**, then turn **L** into car park.

6 Just to **R** of signboard, yellow waymarkers indicate path that passes under trees to **River Tilt**. Turn **R** through exotic **grotto** until wooden steps on **R** lead up to corner of **caravan park**. Head away from river under pines. Ignore track on R and, at corner of **caravan park**, keep ahead under larch trees following faint path. Cross track to take clear path ahead towards **Blair Castle**. Bear **L** at statue of Hercules, passing Hercules Garden (which you may walk round) to front of **castle**.

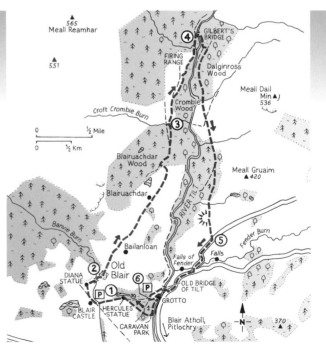

Loch Faskally The Braes o' Killiecrankie

8¾ miles (14.1km) 4hrs **Ascent:** 492ft (150m) ⚠

Paths: Wide riverside paths, minor road, no stiles
Suggested map: OS Explorer 386 Pitlochry & Loch Tummel
Grid reference: NN 917626 **Parking:** Killiecrankie visitor centre

From the battlefield to Loch Faskally.

1 Cross front of **visitor centre** to steps (**'Soldier's Leap'**), leading down into wooded gorge. Footbridge crosses waterfall of Troopers' Den. At next junction, turn **L** ('**Soldier's Leap**'). Ten steps down, spur path on **R** leads to viewpoint above **Soldier's Leap**.

2 Return to main path ('**Linn of Tummel**'), which runs down to join **River Garry** below railway viaduct. After 1 mile (1.6km) it reaches footbridge.

3 Don't cross footbridge, but continue ahead ('**Pitlochry**'), along riverside under tall South Garry road bridge. Path runs around huge river pool to tarred lane; turn **R** here. Lane leaves lochside, then passes track on **R**, blocked by vehicle barrier. Ignore this; shortly turn **R** ('**Pitlochry**').

4 Immediately bear **L** to pass along R-H side of **Loch Dunmore**, following red-top posts. Footbridge crosses **loch**, but turn away from it, half-**R**, on to small path that becomes dirt track. After 110yds (100m) it reaches wider track. Turn **L**, with white/yellow waymarker. After 220yds (201m) track starts to climb; here white/yellow markers indicate smaller path on **R**, which follows lochside. Where it rejoins wider path, bear **R** at green waymarker and cross footbridge to **A9** road bridge.

5 Cross **Loch Faskally** on Clunie footbridge below road's bridge; turn **R**, on to road around **loch**. In 1 mile (1.6km), at top of grass bank on **L**, is **Priest Stone**. After **Clunie power station**, reach car park on **L**. Here sign indicates steep path down to **Linn of Tummel**.

6 Return to road above for ½ mile (800m), to cross grey suspension bridge on **R**. Turn **R**, downstream, to pass above **Linn**. Spur path back **R** returns to falls at lower level, but main path continues along riverside ('**Killiecrankie**'). It bends **L** and goes down wooden steps to **Garry**, then runs upstream and under high road bridge. Take side-path up on to bridge for view of river, then return to follow descending path ('**Pitlochry via Faskally**'). This runs down to bridge, Point **3**. Return upstream to start.

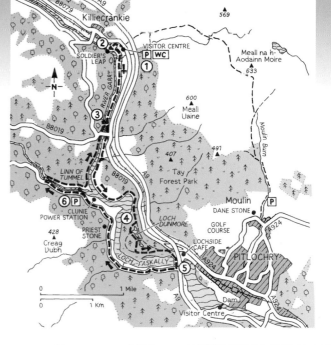

Old Aberdeen Striking Oil in the North Sea

6 miles (9.6km) 2hrs 30min **Ascent:** Neglible ⓞ

Paths: Exellent in all weathers
Suggested map: OS Explorer 406 Aberdeen & Banchory; AA Street by Street Aberdeen
Grid reference: NJ 954067
Parking: Outside Harry Ramsden's on the Esplanade or Queen Link Leisure Park

This walk around the old fishing port celebrates the prosperity and tragedy that oil has brought to Aberdeen.

1 Head southwards on promenade beside shore with sea on **R**. Descend slipway on to beach and continue for short stretch. Step over rocks to reach wooden steps on **R** and leave beach into children's play area.

2 Walk past **Silver Darling restaurant** and into harbour area. Continue past **war memorial**, keeping blue storage tanks on your **L** and along **Pocra Quay**. Turn **L** into **York Street**. At Neptune Bar, turn **L** into **York Place**. Then, take 1st **R**, 1st **L** and 1st **R** again to emerge on **Waterloo Quay**.

3 Where Waterloo Quay becomes **Commerce Street**, turn **L** into **Regent Quay**. At T-junction cross road at pedestrian lights. Turn **L** then 1st **R** to reach **Aberdeen Maritime Museum** and **John Ross's House**.

4 From here, head along Exchequer Row, turn **L** into **Union Street** and turn **R** into **Broad Street**, where you will find **Provost Skene's House**, which dates from 1545, and **Tourist Information Office** on **L**, behind offices.

5 Continue past **Marischal College**; turn **R** into Littlejohn Street, cross **North Street**. At end of Meal Market Street turn **R** into King Street then **L** into Frederick Street. At junction with **Park Street** turn **L** and keep walking until road crosses railway.

6 Shortly after you reach roundabout. Head along **Park Road**, almost straight ahead. Follow it through **cemetery** and towards **Pittodrie Park** and its junction with **Golf Road**.

7 Turn **R** into **Golf Road** and walk through **golf links**. Detour to top of Broad Hill, mound behind cemetery, for magnificent views. Road turns sharply **L** towards its junction with **Esplanade**. Cross **Esplanade**; turn **R** on to promenade, which you follow back to start.

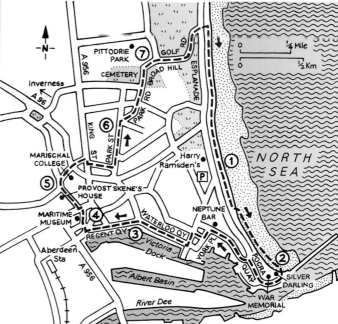

Aberlemno The Mysterious Stones

3 miles (4.8km) 1hr 45min **Ascent:** 394ft (120m)

Paths: Mainly quiet roads but one extremely overgrown area

Suggested map: OS Explorer 389 Forfar, Brechin & Edzell

Grid reference: NO 522558

Parking: Car park by school in Aberlemno

Through land once inhabited by the Picts.

1 From car park turn **R** and walk along road, go 1st **L** ('**Aberlemno** church and stone'). Pass church – famous **Pictish stone** in churchyard – and follow road as it bends **R**. Follow road to T-junction.

2 Turn **R** and follow road, passing entrance to **Woodside** on **L**. At corner, follow road as it bends **R**. Walk down to join B9134, turn **R** and follow this short distance to turning on **L**.

3 Turn **L** along this road ('**Finavon Hill**'), passing house at bottom called Hillcrest. Road winds uphill, past several rocky outcrops, then under line of pylons. Continue as road skirts hill.

4 Continue and soon see **mast**, followed by pond on **L**, and pass hill on **R**, once topped with ancient **fort**. Continue to padlocked gate on **L**. You can make a diversion here. Climb gate and walk up track, passing 2 ponds to reach house.

5 Turn **R** on grassy track and walk back on yourself, going through gate in deer fence, then past several pheasant feeders. Go through another gate at bottom, turn **L** and return to road.

6 After you have completed the loop, turn **R** and retrace your steps back to the start of the walk at **Aberlemno**.

Auchenblae An Inspirational Landscape

4½ miles (7.2km) 2hrs 20min **Ascent:** 459ft (140m)

Paths: Established footpaths, overgrown woodland tracks

Suggested map: OS Explorer 396 Stonehaven, Inverbervie & Lawrencekirk

Grid reference: NO 727787

Parking: On street in Auchenblae

Walk through the Howe of Mearns.

1 With your back to **post office** on main street, turn **R** and cross over to follow signs ('Woodland Walk'). Go down tarmac slope, past play area and over bridge. Follow track uphill, passing woodland on your **R**, continue to road.

2 Turn **R**, walk along long, straight road, passing **cemetery**. Take 1st turning **L**, which runs between arable fields. Continue to wood ahead. Go through rusty gate and scramble through undergrowth to get into woods and join track.

3 Turn **R** and follow track round margin of woods – thickly carpeted with vegetation. At wider gravel track, turn **R** and continue – fields still visible through trees on R-H side. Follow track to crossing of tracks.

4 Take L-H fork. At pylon on R-H side of track, strike off on indistinct track that runs downhill to **R** under line of pylons. (If you go under pylons on main track, you've gone too far.)

5 Scramble through undergrowth and follow indistinct track as it swings to **L**, in northwesterly direction. (I had to negotiate my way past fallen trees at this point, which had been damaged by a recent storm – so be careful, as some of them were large.) Eventually come down to meet main road.

6 Turn **R** and follow road, pass the entrance to **Drumtochty Castle** ('Private Residence'). Continue along road until you reach fork in road.

7 Take L-H fork an continue ahead.

8 Turn **R** along road for few paces, then go **L** at junction and follow road back into Auchenblae. At main street, turn **R** and return to start.

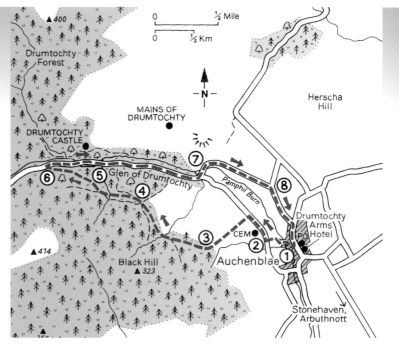

Stonehaven Hidden Treasure

3½ miles (5.7km) 1hr 30min **Ascent:** 377ft (115m)

Paths: Cliff edges, metalled tracks, forest paths, 3 stiles
Suggested map: OS Explorer 273 Stonehaven & Inverbervie
Grid reference: NO 874858
Parking: Market Square, Stonehaven

Along the cliffs to Dunnottar Castle, which once housed Scotland's crown jewels.

❶ From Market Square, walk back on to Allardyce Street, turn **R** and cross road. Turn **L** up Market Lane. At beach, turn **R** to cross footbridge. Turn **R** at signs to **Dunnottar Castle** to reach harbour. Cross here to continue down Shorehead, on east side of harbour. Pass **Marine Hotel**, then turn **R** into Wallis Wynd.

❷ Turn **L** into Castle Street. Emerge at main road then maintain direction walking along road until it bends. Continue ahead, following enclosed tarmac track, between arable fields and past war **memorial** on R-H side. Nip over stile at end of track.

❸ Make your way across middle of field, cross footbridge and 2 more stiles. You now pass track going down to **Castle Haven** and continue following main path around cliff edge. Cross another footbridge and bear uphill. You'll soon reach some steps on your **L** that run down to **Dunnottar Castle**.

❹ Route bears **R** here, past waterfall, through kissing gate and up to house. Pass house to reach road into **Stonehaven** by Mains of Dunnottar, turn **R** then take 1st turning on **L**, walking in direction of radio **masts**. Follow this wide, metalled track past **masts** and East Newtonleys on L-H side, to reach **A957**.

❺ Turn **R** and walk downhill. Take 1st turning on **L**. Follow track to sign on **R** ('Carron Gate'). Turn **R** and walk through woods, following lower path on R-H side that runs by burn. You'll soon reach **Shell House** on **L**.

❻ Pass it on **L**, continue along lower track then climb uphill to join wider track. Bear **R** here, to maintain direction and reach edge of woods. Go through housing estate to join Low Wood Road and river.

❼ Turn **L**, then **R** to cross footbridge with green railings. Turn **R** and walk beside the water. You'll soon pass art-deco **Carron Restaurant** on L-H side, and then come to cream-coloured iron bridge. Bear **L** here then turn 1st **R** to return to Market Square.

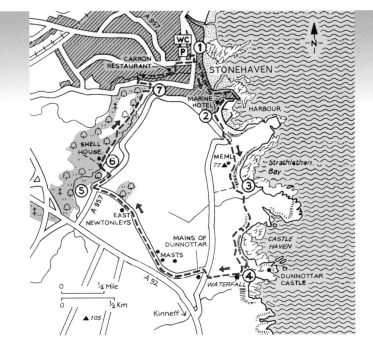

Braemar Moorland on Morrone

6¾ miles (10.9km) 4hrs 15min **Ascent:** 2,000ft (610m)

Paths: Well-made but fairly steep path, track, 1 stile
Suggested map: OS Explorer 387 Glen Shee & Braemar
Grid reference: NO 143911
Parking: Duck Pond, at top of Chapel Brae, Braemar

The hill at the back of Braemar gives a taste of the Cairngorms.

❶ Take wide track uphill, to R of **duck pond** at top of Chapel Brae, bearing **L** twice to **Woodhill** house. House can be bypassed by taking small footpath on **R** which rejoins track just above. When track forks again, bear **L** to viewpoint indicator.

❷ Cross track diagonally to hill path ('**Morrone**') – rebuilt with rough stone steps. Higher up, it slants to **R** along line of rocky outcrops. At top of this it turns directly uphill, passing 5 sprawling **cairns**. These are the turning point in the Morrone Hill Race that is part of the Braemar Games. Wide, stony path runs up to **radio mast** and other ugly constructions on summit.

❸ The summit, with your back to buildings, has fine views across to the **Cairngorms**. On the main tops snow may show in summer. To the east are Loch Callater and White Mouth plateau. The notable hump is Cac Carn Beag, one of the summits of Lochnagar.

Morrone's summit area is bare stones, but if you go past buildings you'll find start of wide track. It runs down to shallow col and climbs to **cairn** on low summit beyond. Here it bends **L** towards lower col, but before reaching it, turns **L** again down hill. Gentle zig-zagging descent leads to road by **Clunie Water**.

❹ Turn **L**, alongside river, for 1½ miles (2.4km). Ben Avon with its row of summit tors fills the skyline ahead. After snow gate and golf **clubhouse** comes road sign warning of cattle grid (grid is round next bend). Here track, back up to **L**, has blue-topped waymarker pole.

❺ Go up between caravans to ladder stile with dog flap. Faint path leads up under birches, bearing **R** and becoming clearer. After gate in fence path becomes quite clear, leading to Scottish Natural Heritage signboard and blue waymarker at top of birchwood. Path becomes track with fence on **R** and, in 220yds (201m), reaches viewpoint indicator, Point ❷. Return to **duck pond**.

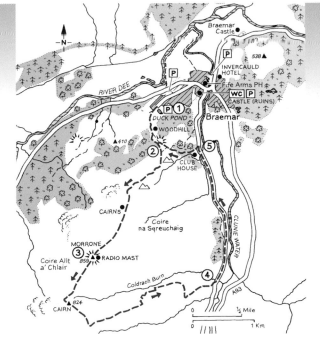

73 Glenlivet The Whisky Hills

6¼ miles (10.1km) 3hrs 15min **Ascent:** 1,000ft (305m) ▲

Paths: Waymarked, muddy and indistinct in places, 11 stiles. Note: Grouse shooting in August/September – consult Glenlivet Ranger Service at Tomintoul

Suggested map: OS Explorer 420 Correen Hills & Glenlivet

Grid reference: NJ 218257

Parking: Track opposite church at Tombae runs up to quarry car park

Through a green valley and heather moor.

❶ At **Tombae** church, turn **L** for 330yds (300m) to stile on **R** ('Walk 10'). Track leads down into birchwoods. Bear **R** at waymark and follow main track to bridge over **River Livet**. After 60yds (55m), turn **R** to bridge over **Crombie Water**. Turn half-**L**, up to stile beside field gate. Walk follows top of low wooded bank above **Crombie Water** to footbridge (grid ref 226245).

❷ Across footbridge, path runs across meadow into wood, slanting up to **R** to green track. Turn **R**; follow this through wood, then bend **L** on to moorland. Below abrupt hill of **The Bochel** track forks. Keep ahead, with waymark. Way becomes peaty path. At top of 1st rise is stile with gate alongside. Path, with waymarker, leads to gateway in another fence. Don't go through, but turn **R**, with fence on your **L**, to stile with signpost.

❸ For easier alternative, follow sign ahead. Just before house, turn **R** at signpost and follow rough

track towards **Bochel** farm. But main route goes over **The Bochel** itself. Across stile, turn uphill on small paths to summit cairn. Turn **L**, to descend towards large white **Braeval distillery** below Ladder Hills. As slope steepens, see **Bochel** farm below. Head down **L-H** edge of nearer pine wood to join rough track leading into farm.

❹ At once stile on **R** leads to faint path into plantation. This becomes green track running just above bottom edge of wood. It becomes more well-used and leads to road.

❺ Turn **R**, over bridge to waymarked stile on **R**. Track rises to open fields above river. At highest point, waymarker points down to **R**. Go down to fence, with waymarked stile on **L**, then through heather with fence on your **L**. Turn downhill to stile at bottom. Cross and turn **L**, ignoring another stile on **L**, to reach footbridge, Point **❷**. Retrace 1st part of walk back to **Tombae**.

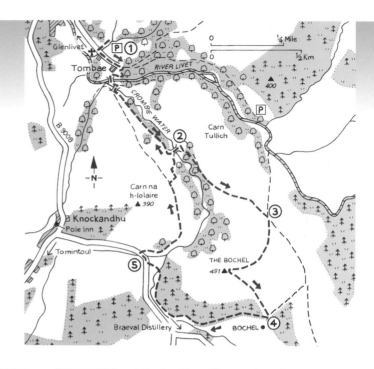

---

74 Fort William Peat Road to Cow Hill

7¼ miles (11.6km) 3hrs 30min **Ascent:** 1,000ft (300m) ▲

Paths: Smooth tracks, 2 stiles

Suggested map: OS Explorer 392 Ben Nevis & Fort William

Grid reference: NN 098736

Parking: Shore Car Park (pay-and-display)

A superb walk, looking down at Fort William and up at Ben Nevis and then home along the glen.

❶ From back corner of car park cross over **A82**, and go up to **R** of **school** to path under trees, and then up to **Lundavra Road**. Turn **R**, going uphill, to top of town. Cross over cattle grid to signed gate on **L** ('Keep Clear 24hr').

❷ The track ahead is the **Peat Road**, once used for hauling peat off the hill on wooden sledges. Follow track past waymarker ('**Peat Road**') to **Cow Hill** summit with radio **mast**. This is the destination of a mid-winter hill race straight up from the town. Return to waymarker.

❸ Turn **L** down path, into forest and head steeply downhill. Cross over track, with **West Highland Way** marker, and then leave forest. On **L** is **burial ground**, reached by short side path through gate. Continue on main path to Glen Nevis road. Turn **L** 100yds (91m)

and then bear **R** on path to **Ionad Nibheis visitor centre**, which has interesting displays on the geology and wildlife of the glen.

❹ Follow river bank past car park to footbridge ('Ben Path'). Cross and then turn **L**, downstream. With road ahead, riverside path forks off **L**. This path is narrow and can sometimes be boggy, but alternatively you can follow road ahead instead. Path and road rejoin after ½ mile (800m) and then continue for 300yds (274m) to green footbridge on **L**.

❺ Cross and turn **R**, down track then road, to roundabout. Turn **L** along pavement into **Fort William**. In front of station, pass underpass entrance (or go **L** through underpass for shopping shortcut to walk start). Bear **R** past front of station and through Safeway car park, and cross roundabout to **Old Fort**. This is the original **Fort William**, and the start point of the Great Glen Way. Turn **L** on pavement above **Loch Linnhe**, to car park.

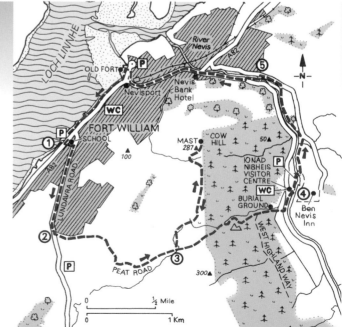

Corpach The Banks of the Caledonian Canal

4½ miles (7.2km) 1hr 45min **Ascent:** 100ft (30m)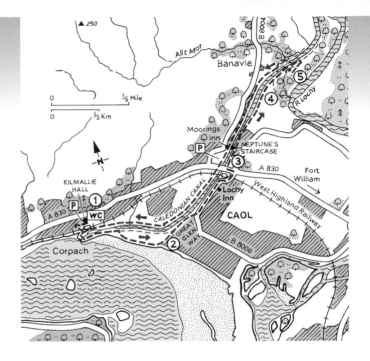
Paths: Wide tow paths, no stiles
Suggested map: OS Explorer 392 Ben Nevis & Fort William
Grid reference: NN 097768
Parking: Kilmallie Hall, Corpach

A walk alongside and underneath Thomas Telford's masterpiece.

❶ Go down past **Corpach** Station to **canal** and cross sea lock that separates salt water from fresh water. Follow **canal** (on L) up past another lock, where path on R has blue footpath sign and **Great Glen Way** marker. It passes under sycamores to shore. Follow shoreline path past football pitch. Turn **L**, across grass to road sign warning motorists of nearby playground. Path ahead leads up wooded bank to tow path.

❷ Turn **R** along tow path, for ½ mile (800m). Just before **Banavie** swing bridge, path down to **R** has **Great Glen Way** marker. Follow waymarkers on street signs to level crossing then turn **L** towards other swing bridge, one with road on it.

❸ Just before bridge, turn **R** at signs for **Great Glen Way** and the Great Glen Cycle Route and continue along tow path to **Neptune's Staircase**. The 60ft (18m) of ascent alongside 8 locks is the serious uphill

part of this walk, but more serious for boats. It takes about 90 minutes to work through the system.

❹ Gate marks top of locks. About 200yds (183m) later, grey gate on R leads to dump for dead cars; ignore this one. Over next 100yds (91m) **canal** crosses little wooded valley, with black fence on R. Now comes 2nd grey gate. Go through, to track turning back sharp **R** and descending to cross stream.

❺ On R, stream passes right under **canal** in arched tunnel, and alongside is 2nd tunnel which provides a walkers' way to other side. Water from the **canal** drips into the tunnel (it's a bit spooky) – try not to think of the large boats sailing directly over your head! At end, track runs up to join **canal's** northern tow path. Turn **R**, back down tow path. After passing **Neptune's Staircase**, cross **A830** to level crossing without warning lights. Continue ahead along **R-H** tow path. After 1 mile (1.6km) tow path track leads back to **Corpach** double lock.

Grantown-on-Spey Sir James Grant's Town

7 miles (11.3km) 3hrs **Ascent:** 200ft (60m)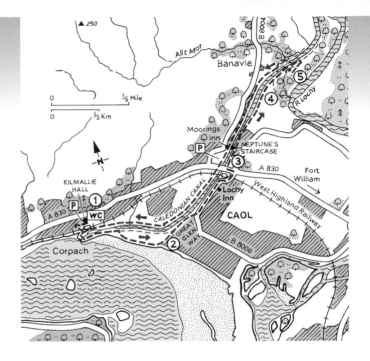
Paths: Tracks and smooth paths, 1 stile
Suggested map: OS Explorer 419 Grantown-on-Spey
Grid reference: NJ 035280
Parking: Grantown-on-Spey Museum

Around an 18th-century planned town.

❶ Go past **museum**. Turn **L** into South Street, then **R** into Golf Course Road. Tarred path crosses **golf course** to gate into **Anagach Wood**.

❷ Wide path ahead has blue/red waymarker. At junction, blue trail departs to R; turn **L**, following **Spey Way** marker and red-top poles. Keep following red markers, turning **L** at 1st junction and bearing **L** at next. When track joins new fence and bend in stream is on L, keep ahead, following **Spey Way** marker.

❸ Track emerges into open fields. After crossing small bridge, turn to **R** through chained gap stile. Path with pines on its L leads to track near **River Spey**. (**Bridge of Cromdale** is just ahead.)

❹ Turn sharp **R** on track, alongside river. At fishers' hut it re-enters forest. About ¾ mile (1.2km) later it diminishes to green path and slants up past cottage of **Craigroy** to join its entrance track.

❺ At **Easter Anagach**, grass track on R has red

waymarkers and runs into birchwood. With barrier ahead, follow marker poles to **L**, on to broad path beside falling fence. At next junction, turn **R**, following red poles, over slight rise. Descending, turn **L** just before blue-top post, on to smaller path with blue-and-red posts. This runs along top of ridge, to reach bench above lane. Down the lane is the stone bridge built as part of the military road system.

❻ Path bends **R**, alongside road, to meet wide track (former military road). Turn **R**, to path on R with green-top posts. At small pool, main path bends **L** for 150yds (137m), with blue-and-green posts; take path ahead, with green posts. A very old tree in the middle of the path was once used for public hangings. At 5-way junction bear **L** to find next green post. At edge of **golf course** turn **L** to car park and information board.

❼ Follow tarred street uphill, past end of **golf course**, to High Street. Turn **R** to The Square. Just past Grant Arms Hotel, sign points **R**, to **museum**.

Shieldaig Loch-side Shores

3¼ miles (5.3km) 1hr 45min **Ascent:** 500ft (152m) ⚠
Paths: Well-made old paths, 1 rough section
Suggested map: OS Explorer 428 Kyle of Lochalsh
Grid reference: NG 814538
Parking: South end of Shieldaig village, opposite shop and hotel

In the footsteps of Bonnie Prince Charlie around the inlets of the Shieldaig peninsula.

❶ Follow village street along shoreline. At village end it rises slightly, with another parking area, and **war memorial** above on R.

❷ From front of **school**, turn R up rough track. Track passes 2 houses to turn L. In another 100yds (91m) it divides and here main track for **Rubha Lodge** forks off L, but your route bears R, passing to R of glacier-smoothed rock knoll. Terraced path runs through birch woods at first, with **Loch Shieldaig** below (L). It passes above 2 rocky bays then strikes across peat bog. In middle of this flat area it divides at cairn.

❸ R-H path runs along L edge of peaty area, with rocky ground above on its L, then next to birch trees for 50yds (46m). Look out for point where its pink gravel surface becomes peaty, with rock formation like low ruin on R, because here there is easily-missed path junction.

❹ What appears to be main footpath, ahead and slightly downhill, peters out eventually. Correct path forks off to **L**, slanting up on to higher ground just above. Path is now clear, crossing slabby ground in direction of peninsula's **trig point**, ¼ mile (400m) away. After 220yds (201m) it rises slightly to gateway in former fence. Aiming **R** of **trig point**, it crosses small heather moor. At broken wall, path turns down **R** through gap to top of grassy meadow. Shoreline cottage, **Bad-callda**, is just below. Rough paths lead to **L** across boggy top of meadow and above birchwood, with trig point just above on L. Keep going forward at same level to heather knoll, with pole on it. Just below you is 2nd cottage, **Camas-ruadh**.

❺ Footpath zig-zags down between rocks. White paint spots lead round to **R** of cottage, to join clear path coming from cottage. Return path is easy to follow, with cottage's phone line always near by on L. After ½ mile (800m) it rejoins outward route at **cairn**.

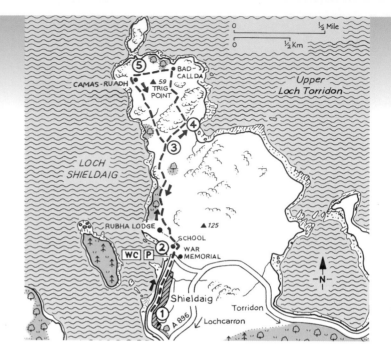

Glen Coe Into the Lost Valley

2¾ miles (4.4km) 2hrs 15min **Ascent:** 1,050ft (320m) ⚠
Paths: Rugged and stony, stream to wade through, 1 stile
Suggested map: OS Explorer 384 Glen Coe & Glen Etive
Grid reference: NN 168569
Parking: Lower of two roadside parking places opposite Gearr Aonach (middle one of Three Sisters)

A rugged waterfall walk.

❶ From uphill corner of car park, faint path slants down to old road, which is now well-used track. Head up-valley for 650yds (594m). With old road continuing as green track ahead, your path now bends down to R. Path reaches gorge of **River Coe**. Descend on steep wooden step ladder to cross footbridge.

❷ Ascent out of gorge is on bare rock staircase. Above, path runs through regenerating birch wood which can be wet on legs. Cross high ladder stile over temporary fence. Path runs uphill for 60yds (55m). Here it bends L; inconspicuous alternative path continues uphill, which can be used to bypass narrow path of main route.

❸ Main route contours into gorge of **Allt Coire Gabhail**. It is narrow with steep drops below. Where there is alternative of rock slabs and narrow path just below, slabs are more secure. Two fine **waterfalls** come into view ahead. Pass these, continue between boulders to where main path bends L to cross stream below boulder size of small house. (Ignore small path which runs on up to R of stream.) River here is wide and fairly shallow, 5 or 6 **stepping stones** usually allow dry crossing. If water is above stones, it's safer to wade alongside them; if water is more than knee-deep crossing should not be attempted.

❹ Well-built path continues uphill, now with stream on R. After 100yds (91m) rock blocks way. Path follows slanting ramp up its R-H side. It continues uphill, passing above boulder pile that blocks valley. At top of rock pile path levels, giving view into Lost Valley.

❺ Drop gently to valley's gravel floor. Stream vanishes into gravel, to reappear below boulder pile on other side. Note where path arrives at gravel, as it becomes invisible at that point. Wander up valley to where stream vanishes, ¼ mile (400m) ahead. Beyond this point is more serious hillwalking. Return to path and follow it back to start.

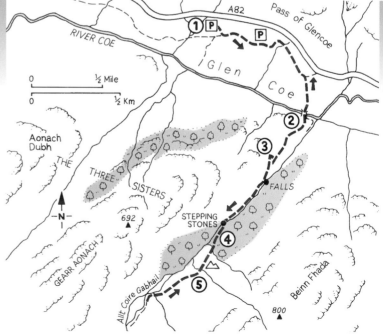

Glen Coe Around the Small Shepherd

8 miles (12.9km) 4hrs 30min Ascent: 1,300ft (396m) ▲3
Paths: Rough, unmade paths, some boggy bits, no stiles. Note: Fords in Lairig Eilde can be impassible or dangerous after heavy rain
Suggested map: OS Explorer 384 Glen Coe & Glen Etive
Grid reference: NN 213559
Parking: Large parking area on south side of A82, marked by yellow AA phone post

Through the mountains.

❶ Signpost to Glen Etive, at edge of car park, marks start of path into **Lairig Gartain**. Path, clear but boggy in places, heads up-valley with **River Coupall** down on L. Gradually it draws closer to river, but does not cross it. Large cairn marks top of path, which is slightly to R of lowest point of pass.

❷ Descending path is steeper, over boggy grass with new stream forming on L. After ½ mile (800m), ignore small path branching off L towards waterfall below, and stay on main, higher path. This slants along R-H wall of valley, ascending above stream. Eventually emerge on to steep south ridge of **Stob Dubh**.

❸ Here path runs down to gate in deer fence, but do not continue downhill. Follow faint path above deer fence, descending to cross **Allt Lairig Eilde**. If stream is too full to cross, return and go down through deer fence to wider, shallower crossing, 200yds (183m)

downstream. Alternatively, head up on small path to **R** of stream, to find safer crossing higher up. Across stream, follow fence up to gate at its corner. Turn up wide path that rises out of Glen Etive.

❹ Path ascends to L of stream, passing waterfalls. Eventually cross stream, now smaller, then continue straight ahead, crossing col well to R of its lowest point. Large cairn marks top of path.

❺ New, descending stream is also, confusingly, **Allt Lairig Eilde**. Path crosses it by wide, shallow ford and goes down its L bank. 1 mile (1.6km) ahead, path recrosses via boulder **stepping stones**. It runs down to join **A82** near **cairn** that marks entry into **Glen Coe**.

❻ Cross road, and river beyond, to join **old Glencoe road** at arched culvert. Turn **R** along firm track, which soon rejoins new road, then cross diagonally, on to damp path. This runs to R of new road, then recrosses. It soon rejoins **A82** opposite start.

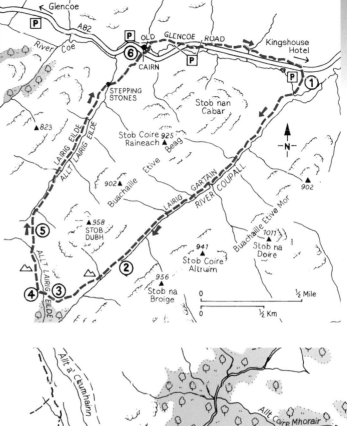

Kinlochleven Grey Mare's Tail

3½ miles (5.7km) 2hrs 15min Ascent: 984ft (300m) ▲2
Paths: Well-made paths, one steep, rough ascent, no stiles
Suggested map: OS Explorer 384 Glen Coe & Glen Etive or 392 Ben Nevis & Fort William
Grid reference: NN 187622 (on Explorer 384) **Parking:** Grey Mare's Tail car park, Kinlochleven

A ramble down the West Highland Way.

❶ Smooth gravel path leads up out of car park to multicoloured waymarks pointing **L**. Path rises to view through trees of **Grey Mare's Tail** waterfall, then descends to footbridge. Here turn **L** (blue waymarker) to visit foot of spectacular waterfall, then return to take path on **R** (white, yellow and green waymarker). Follow stream up for 100yds (91m), then turn **L** at waymarker. Path, steep and loose, zig-zags up through birches to more open ground.

❷ Where path forks take **R-H** branch, with yellow-and-green waymarker, to pass under power lines. Path follows crest of heathery spur, then bends **L** to cross 2 streams. Immediately after 2nd stream is another junction.

❸ Confusing waymarker has 8 arrows in 4 colours. Turn **L**, following white arrow slightly downhill, to cross footbridge above waterfall and red granite rocks. Path leads up under birches. Ground cover here includes the aromatic bog myrtle, which can be used to

discourage midges, though it is less effective than chemical repellent. When path reaches track, turn **L** (white arrow). Below track is tin deer used by stalkers for target practice. Signed footpath bypasses **Keepers' Cottages** on L, then rejoins track beyond, to junction above **Mamore Lodge**.

❹ Keep ahead, above lodge, climbing gently past 2 tin huts, self-catering accommodation labelled 'stable' and 'bothy'. At high point of track there is TV **mast** on R and bench on L. Track descends gently, with slabs of quartzite above. Wide path of **West Highland Way (WHW)** can be seen below and gradually rises to join track, with large waymarker planted in cairn.

❺ Turn **L** down **WHW** path, which drops into woods below. Watch out for junction where main path seems to double back to R; take smaller path, continuing ahead with **WHW** waymarker. After crossing tarred access track of **Mamore Lodge**, path fords small stream to reach village. Turn **L** along pavement and fork **L** into Wades Road to regain car park.

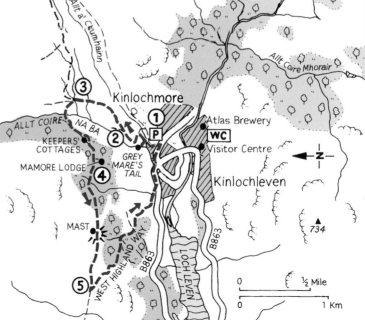

Strontian The Elements of Chemistry

7 miles (11.3km) 3hrs 45min **Ascent:** 950ft (290m) **2**
Paths: Good through woodland, sketchy on open hill, no stiles
Suggested map: OS Explorer 391 Ardgour & Strontian
Grid reference: NM 826633
Parking: Nature Reserve car park at Ariundle

To the site of an old lead mine.

1 From car park, go along track into oakwoods. After ½ mile (800m), footpath turns off at waymarker on **R**. It crosses **Strontian River** and heads upstream along it. After ¾ mile (1.2km) it recrosses **river**, following duckboard section to rejoin oakwood track.

2 Turn **R**, away from car park, to reach high gate in deer fence. Track immediately forks. Take downward branch on **R** to emerge into open grazing at **river** level. Track ends at gate and stream.

3 Ford stream on to rough path. This crosses 3 more small streams, then forks. The lower, R-H branch continues alongside **Strontian River**, but path, which is quite faint, slants up to **L** to solitary holly tree. Here it turns straight uphill for 50yds (46m), then bends **R** to slant up as before, passing 200yds (183m) below bare rock knoll. Remains of wooden steps are in path and few cairns stand beside it. It steepens slightly to pass below small crag with 3 different trees growing

out of it – rowan, hazel and oak. With large stream and **waterfalls** ahead, path turns uphill and reaches brink of small gorge. Above waterfalls, slope eases and there is footbridge down on R which you don't cross; it acts as useful landmark. Just above, path reaches broken dam wall of former reservoir.

4 Green path runs across slope just above. You can turn **R** on this, heading up beside stream for about ¼ mile (400m). Here you will find spoil heap; heather bank marks entrance to an **adit** – mine tunnel.

5 Return along green path past Point **4**, with remains of **Bellsgrove Lead Mines** above and below. Path improves into track, following stream down small and slantwise side valley. As this stream turns down to L, track contours forward, to cross wooded stream valley by high footbridge above **waterfall**.

6 Wide, smooth track continues through gate. After ½ mile (800m) it rejoins outward route at edge of **nature reserve**. Follow track back to car park.

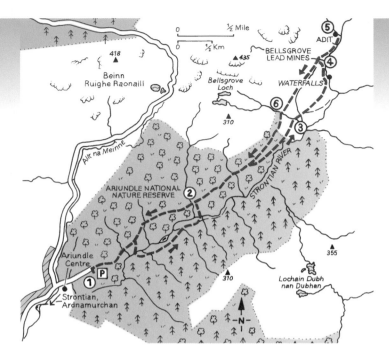

Nevis Gorge Great Falls

2½ miles (4km) 1hr 30min **Ascent:** 270ft (82m) **1**
Paths: Well-built path with drops alongside, no stiles
Suggested map: OS Explorer 392 Ben Nevis & Fort William
Grid reference: NN 168691
Parking: Walkers' car park at end of Glen Nevis road

A walk beside Scotland's Himalayan lookalike leading to an enormous waterfall.

1 It should be noted that waterslide above car park is Allt Coire Eoghainn – if you mistake it for **Steall Fall** and set off towards it you are on difficult and potentially dangerous path. The path you will take on this walk is much easier, but even here there have been casualties, mostly caused by people wearing unsuitable shoes. At top end of car park you will see signpost that shows no destination closer than 13 miles (21km) to Kinlochleven – accordingly, this walk will be short out-and-back. The well-made path runs gently uphill under woods of birch and hazel, across what turns into very steep slope. For few steps it becomes rock-cut ledge, with step across waterfall side-stream. The path at this point is on clean pink granite, but you will see boulder of grey schist beside path just afterwards. Ahead, top of **Steall Fall** can now be seen through notch of valley.

2 The path continues briefly downhill to cross 2nd stream; rock now is schist, with fine zig-zag stripes of grey and white. Short rock staircase leads to wooden balcony section. From here path is just above bed of **Nevis Gorge**. The river runs through huge boulders, some of which bridge it completely.

3 Quite suddenly, path emerges on to level meadow above gorge. Ahead, **Steall Fall** fills your view. The best path runs along **L-H** edge of meadow to point opposite waterfall.

4 The walk ends here, beside footbridge, which consists simply of 3 steel cables over a very deep pool. Those who wish to attempt crossing should note that it gets wobblier in middle and it is hard to turn around, but the return journey is rather easier. From wire bridge, driest path runs alongside main river round 1 bend before heading up to foot of waterfall. The view from directly beneath the waterfall is even more spectacular – enjoy.

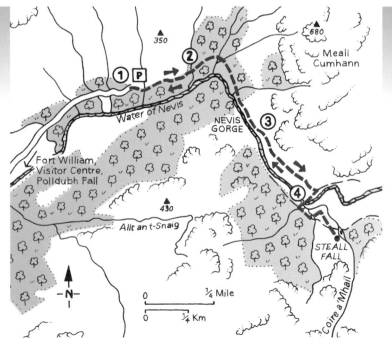

Ben Nevis Half-way Up

10 miles (16.1km) 6hrs 15min **Ascent:** 2,000ft (610m)
Paths: Hill paths, well built, then very rough, 6 stiles
Suggested map: OS Explorer 392 Ben Nevis & Fort William
Grid reference: NN 123731 **Parking:** Large car park at Glen Nevis Visitor Centre

The great north corrie of Nevis.

❶ At downstream corner of car park, bridge ('Ben Path') crosses **River Nevis**. Path turns upstream, crossing fields to join **Mountain Trail** (formerly Pony Track) to Ben Nevis. After long climb, notice points you to zig-zag up **L** on to half-way plateau. Path passes above **Lochan Meall an-t-Suidhe**, Halfway Lochan, down on **L**.

❷ Main path takes sharp turn back to **R**, heading for summit. Your smaller path descends ahead, behind wall-like cairn. Soon it climbs gently over peat bog to cairn on skyline. Here it becomes rough and rocky as it slants down across steep slide slope of valley of **Allt a' Mhuilinn**. Eventually it joins stream and runs up beside it to Charles Inglis Clark (**CIC**) Hut.

❸ Return for 100yds (91m); cross stream on **R** to join path downhill. This descends rocky step with waterslide and reaches ladder stile into plantations.

❹ Go down forest road and where it bends **L** over bridge, keep ahead down rough path. Stay beside stream to ladder stile at railbed. Turn **L** for ½ mile (800m), when side-track joins from **L** and track passes under power lines. In 220yds (201m) take smaller track on **R** that rejoins **Allt a' Mhuilinn**. Keep to **R** of distillery buildings to reach **A82**.

❺ Cross River Lochy on **Victoria Bridge** opposite and turn **L** into fenced-off side road and **L** along street. It rises to railway bridge. Turn **L** on to long footbridge back across Lochy. At end, turn **R** over stile for riverside path. Pass to **R** of rugby ground, then enter woodland. After 2 footbridges, bear **L** on smaller path to edge of **Inverlochy**. Turn **R**, then **L** into street with copper beeches. This leads through Montrose Square to **A82**.

❻ Take street opposite ('Ben Nevis Footpath'). Shortly, take stone bridge to Glen Nevis road. Turn **L** for ¼ mile (400m) to track on **L**. Recross **Nevis** on green footbridge and turn **R** to lay-by ('No Overnight Parking'). Just beyond this small riverside footpath leads up-river to footbridge at **visitor centre**.

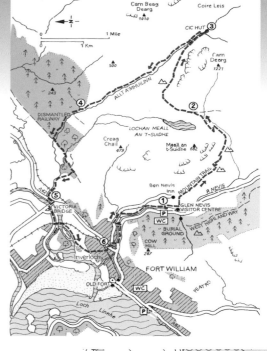

Coire Ardair Happy Birch-day

8 miles (12.9km) 4hrs 15min **Ascent:** 1,400ft (427m)
Paths: Mostly good, wet and stony in places, no stiles
Suggested map: OS Explorer 401 Loch Laggan & Creag Meagaidh
Grid reference: NN 483872
Parking: Nature reserve car park at Aberarder track end beside Loch Laggan

Regenerating woodlands lead to a high pass.

❶ Take gravel track to **Aberarder** farm. (Information area and covered picnic table.) Pass to **R** of buildings following footprint waymarker on to rebuilt path.

❷ Path rises through bracken, then crosses boggy area on old railway sleepers. It heads up valley of **Allt Coire Ardair**, keeping little way up **R-H** side, becoming fairly rocky and rugged as it ascends through area of regenerating birch trees. Crags of **Coire Ardair** come into sight ahead. Path crosses many streams then bends **L**, slightly downhill, to join main river. Peaty area, crossed on railway sleepers, leads up suddenly to outflow of **Lochan a' Choire**.

❸ Outflow is fine viewpoint for crag walls of **Coire Ardair**. These walls are too loose and overgrown for rock climbing, but when covered in snow and hoarfrost give excellent sport for winter mountaineers. The circuit of **lochan** is considerably more rugged than path up glen, and can be omitted if outflow stream is too full, or if you just wish to picnic. Cross outflow stream near where it emerges from **lochan** and follow small path round shore to notable clump of boulders marked by stretcher box. (The stretcher is used for removing mountain casualties from the foot of the crags.) One of boulders forms small cave, with spring running through it. A vigorous rowan tree, seeded where deer can't get at it, shows that without grazing pressure this glen would be wooded even at this altitude of 2,000ft (610m).

❹ After boulder cave you must cross rocks and scree. This short section is awkward so take care. Once past head of **lochan**, slant up away from shore. Path descends from high on **L**, coming out of notch called Window. Join this and turn down to loch's outflow (Point ❸ again). Quite clearly there's no way out of this dead-end valley that doesn't involve serious mountain walking – or one of those winter climbs up icy gullies. Return down valley by outward path.

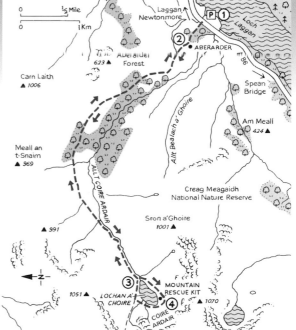

85 Fort Augustus Up and Down the Corrieyairack

7¼ miles (11.7km) 4hrs Ascent: 1,300ft (395m) ③
Paths: Tracks, one vanished pathless section, 2 stiles
Suggested map: OS Explorer 400 Loch Lochy & Glen Roy
Grid reference: NH 378080
Parking: Southern edge of Fort Augustus, signed lane leads off A82 to burial ground

On the road the English built.

❶ Track leads round to **L** of **burial ground** to meet minor road. Turn **R** for ¼ mile (400m) to foot of rubbly track ('Corrieyairack Pass'). After 50yds (46m) track passes through gate, getting easier; soon, right of way joins smoother track coming up from **Culachy House**.

❷ After ¼ mile (400m), gate leads on to hill. 350yds (320m) further on, track passes under high-tension wires. Here bear **L** across meadow. As this drops towards stream, see green track slanting down to R. Bear **L** off track to pass corner of deer fence, where path continues to stream. Cross and turn downstream on grassy track. It recrosses stream and passes under high power line to bend with view across **Glen Tarff**.

❸ Turn **R** across stone bridge. Disused track climbs through birch woods then, as terraced shelf, across high side of **Glen Tarff**. A side stream forms wooded re-entrant ahead. Old track contours into this and crosses below waterfall (former bridge has gone).

❹ Contour out across steep slope to pick up old track as it restarts. It runs uphill to gateless gateway in fence. Turn up fence to another gateway, 150yds (137m) above. Turn **L** for 20yds (18m) to brink of stream hollow. Don't go into this, but turn uphill alongside it, through pathless bracken, to top. Deer fence is just above; turn **L** alongside it to go through nearby gate, then **L** beside fence. When it turns downhill, green path keeps ahead, uphill. Ahead and above, pylons crossing skyline mark Corrieyairack Pass. Path bends **R** to join Corrieyairack track just above.

❺ Turn **R**. Track passes knoll on R where cairn marks highest point. It descends for 1¼ miles (2km). Pass is technically road, and where it crosses stream, Highways Authority sign warns motorists coming up it of difficulties and dangers ahead. From here track climbs gently to rejoin upward route. At final bend, stile offers short cut through ancient **burial ground**.

86 Loch an Eilein Castle on the Island

4¼ miles (6.8km) 1hr 45min Ascent: 100ft (30m) ①
Paths: Wide smooth paths, optional steep hill with high ladder stile
Suggested map: OS Explorer 403 Cairn Gorm & Aviemore
Grid reference: NH 897084
Parking: Estate car park near Loch an Eilein

The castle on the island in the loch is the heart of Rothiemurchus Forest.

❶ From end of car park at beginning of walk, made-up path leads to **visitor centre**. Turn **L** to cross end of **Loch an Eilein**, then turn **R** on smooth sandy track. Loch shore is near by on R. Small paths lead down to it if you wish to visit. Just past red-roofed house, **Forest Cottage**, deer fence runs across, with gate.

❷ Track becomes wide, smooth path, which runs close to loch side. After bridge, main track forks **R** to pass bench backed by flat boulder. Smaller path on **L** leads high into hills and through pass of Lairig Ghru, eventually to Braemar. After crossing stream at low concrete footbridge, path bends **R** for 120yds (110m) to junction. Just beyond is footbridge with handrails.

❸ To shorten walk, cross footbridge and continue along main track, passing Point **❹** in 170yds (155m). For longer walk, turn **L** before footbridge on to narrower path to pass around **Loch Gamhna**. This

2nd loch soon appears on your R-H side. Where path forks, keep **R** to pass along loch side, across its head (rather boggy) and back along its further side, to rejoin wider path around **Loch an Eilein**. Turn **L** here.

❹ Continue around **Loch an Eilein**, water on your R, to reedy corner of loch and bench. About 55yds (51m) further, path turns sharply **R** ('footpath'). After gate, turn **R** to loch side and **memorial** to Major General Brook Rice. Follow shore to point opposite **castle**, then back up to wide track above. Deer fence on **L** leads back to **visitor centre**.

❺ From here, stiff climb (around 500ft/152m) can be made on to rocky hill of **Ord Ban**, superb viewpoint. Cross ladder stile immediately to R of toilets and follow deer fence to **R** for 150yds (137m), to point behind car park. Just behind one of lowest birches on slope, small path zig-zags up steep slope. It slants to **L** to avoid crags, then crosses small rock slab (take care if wet) and continues to summit. Descend by same path.

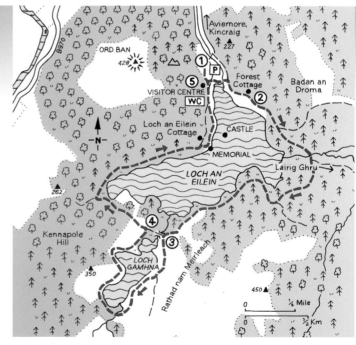

Glenmore The Thieves' Road

5 miles (8km) 2hrs 15min **Ascent:** 400ft (122m) ▲
Paths: Smooth tracks, one steep ascent, no stiles
Suggested map: OS Explorer 403 Cairn Gorm & Aviemore
Grid reference: NH 080005 Parking: Bridge just south of Glenmore village

To the lochan, once the haunt of fairy folk.

❶ Head upstream on sandy track to L of river. Interpretation signs explain the flowers of the forest – there are many ferns and mosses. After 550yds (503m), turn L on wide smooth path (blue/yellow waymarkers). Ahead is gate into **Glenmore Lodge** rifle range; here path bends R, to wide gravel track.

❷ Turn R, away from **Glenmore Lodge**, to cross over concrete bridge into **Caledonian Reserve**. Immediately keep straight ahead on smaller track (blue waymarker) as main one bends R. Track narrows as it heads into **Pass of Ryvoan** between steep wooded slopes of pine, birch and scree. At sign that warns of end of waymarking, path turns L (blue waymarker), which you take in a moment. Just beyond, steps on R lead down to **Lochan Uaine**. Walk round to L of water on beach. At head of loch small path leads back up to track. Turn sharp L, back to junction already visited and now turn off to R on to narrower path (blue waymarker).

❸ This small path crosses duckboard and heads back down valley. Very soon it starts to climb steeply to R, up rough stone steps. When it levels going is easier, although it's still narrow with tree roots. Path reaches forest road at bench and waymarker.

❹ Continue to L along track. After clear-felled area with views, track re-enters trees and slopes downhill into **Glenmore** village. Just above main road turn R, through green barrier, to reach **Glenmore Visitor Centre**. Pass through car park to main road.

❺ Cross to Glenmore shop (café). Behind red postbox, steps lead down to campsite. Pass along its R-H edge to wide path into birch woods (blue/brown waymarkers). Head L across footbridge to shore of **Loch Morlich** and follow beaches (or paths in woods on L) until another river blocks way. Turn L along river bank. Ignore footbridge, but continue on wide path (brown/blue waymarkers) with river on your R. Where path divides, smaller branch (blue waymarkers) continues beside river through bushes to car park.

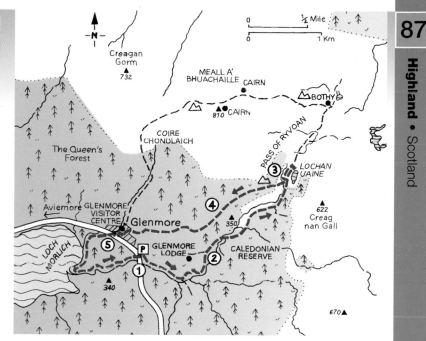

Glenelg Over the Sea to Skye

7¼ miles (11.7km) 3hrs 30min **Ascent:** 750ft (228m) ▲
Paths: Tracks, grassy shoreline, minor road, no stiles
Suggested map: OS Explorer 413 Knoydart, Loch Hourn & Loch Duich
Grid reference: NG 795213
Parking: Above pier of Glenelg ferry

Along the coast with views to Skye.

❶ Track runs out of car park ('Ardintoul and Totaig'), ascends gently through 2 gates, then through 3rd into plantation. With high power lines just above, track forks. Take L-H one, downhill, passing arrow painted on rock. Track runs between feet of pylon then climbs through birch wood. It runs in and out of tiny stream gorge, then descends towards shore. On other side of **Loch Alsh**, houses of Balmacara are directly ahead.

❷ At shoreline, track disappears into open field strip. Follow short-cropped grass next to shingle beach, passing salmon farm just offshore. When trees once more run down to sea, green track runs next to shore. It passes below small crag with birches to reach open flat ground near **Ardintoul Farm**. Keep along shore, outside field walls, sometimes taking to stripy schist shingle, towards square brick building on point ahead. Before reaching it you come to wall gap. Here track, pair of green ruts, runs directly inland. It

joins gravel track, where you turn L to pass sheds and house to regain shoreline at Ardintoul.

❸ Track runs along shoreline, then turns inland to climb hill. Steeper uphill sections are tarred. Below on L, **Allt na Dalach** runs into Loch Alsh, with clear example of gravel spit where river debris runs into tidal water. Track enters plantations, crosses stream and bends R to complete climb to **Bealach Luachrach**. You may see fresh peat workings on L.

❹ Divert here on to **Glas Bheinn** – a tough hill, but a fine viewpoint. (Grading and timing don't take account of side-trip.) From road's high point, turn R up wet tree gap to reach hillside. Follow remains of old fence up first rise. Where it bends R, continue uphill to summit, returning by same route. Use old fence to guide you back into tree gap. Continue downhill from Point ❹ on unsurfaced road, which reaches tarred public road 1 mile (1.6km) north of **Glenelg**. Grassy verge between road and sea leads back to ferry pier.

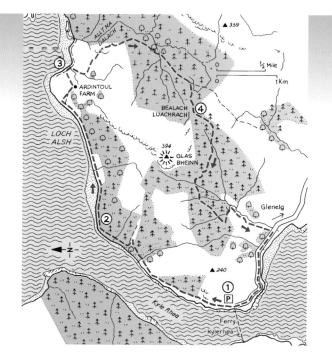

89 | Glenbrittle Heart of the Cuillins

5¾ miles (9.2km) 4hrs **Ascent:** 1,900ft (580m) ⓶
Paths: Mountain paths, one boggy and tough, 2 stiles
Suggested map: OS Explorer 411 Skye – Cuillin Hills
Grid reference: NG 409206
Parking: Walkers' pull-off before gate into Glenbrittle campsite

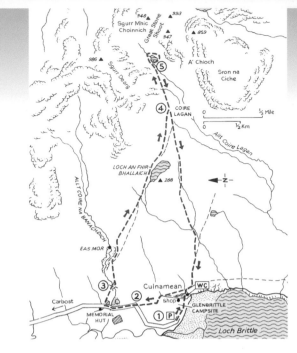

Classic rock climbing country.

❶ From parking area, track leads on through **Glenbrittle campsite** to gate with kissing gate. Pass to L of toilet block to cross stile. Turn **L** along stony track just above, which runs gently downhill above **campsite**, to rejoin Glenbrittle road.

❷ Continue over bridge with white **Memorial Hut** just ahead. On R are stone buchts (sheep-handling enclosures) and here waymarked path heads uphill to reach footbridge over **Allt Coire na Banachdich**.

❸ Cross footbridge and head up to **R** of stream's deep ravine. Look out for short side-path on **L** for best view of waterfall. Above, path bears **R**, to slant up hillside. This part of path has never been built or repaired and is bog and boulder. It passes above **Loch an Fhir-bhallaich** and forks, with **L-H** higher branch being drier but with loose eroded scree. It rounds shoulder into lower part of **Coire Lagan** and meets much larger and better path.

❹ Turn uphill on this path, until belt of bare rock blocks way into upper corrie. This rock has been smoothed by a glacier into gently-rounded swells, known as 'boiler-plates'. Scree field runs up into boiler-plate rocks. Best route keeps up **L** edge, below slab wall with small waterslide, to highest point of scree. Head up **L** for few steps on bare rock, then back **R** on ledges to an eroded scree above boiler-plate obstruction. Look back down your upward route to note it for your return. Trodden way slants up to **R**. With main stream near by on **R**, it goes up to rim of upper corrie.

❺ Boiler-plate slabs at lochan's outflow are excellent for picnics. Walking mainly on bare rock, it's easy to make circuit of lochan. For return journey, retrace your steps to Point ❹. Ignoring R fork of route you came up by, keep straight downhill on main path. It runs straight down to toilet block at **Glenbrittle campsite** at start.

90 | Quiraing Prison and Pinnacle

5¼ miles (8.4km) 3hrs **Ascent:** 1,200ft (365m) ⓷
Paths: Well-used path, 1 stile
Suggested map: OS Explorer 408 Skye – Trotternish & the Storr
Grid reference: NG 440679
Parking: Pull-in, top of pass on Staffin–Uig road. Overflow parking at cemetery ¼ mile (400m) on Staffin side (not during funerals)

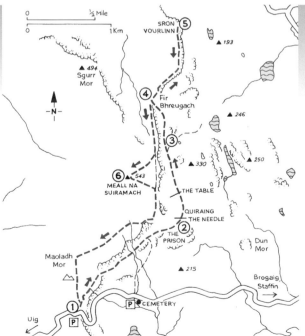

Skye's northern peninsula's lava landscape.

❶ Well-built path starts at 'bendy road' sign opposite lay-by. Jagged tower of grass and rock on skyline is **the Prison**. Path crosses steep landslip slope towards it, with awkward crossing of small stream gully on bare rock, then passes small waterfall high above and heads to **R** rather than up into rocky gap. It turns uphill into wide col to L of **the Prison**.

❷ Main path does not drop, but goes forward, slightly uphill, crossing old fence line at crag foot. It crosses foot of steep ground, then passes above small peat pool. Ignore path forking down R; main path slants up **L** into col where old wall runs across.

❸ Path descends into landslip valley that runs across hillside, then slants up **L** to col with stile.

❹ Cross and turn **R** for excursion to **Sron Vourlinn**. Follow crest over slightly rocky section with short descent beyond, then join main path along grassy meadow with sudden edge on R. After highest point, continue slightly downhill to north top. Here see that land is still slipping, with crevasse beside cliff edge where another narrow section is shortly to peel away.

❺ Return to col with stile (Point ❹) and continue uphill. Drops are now on L, as you look down towards pinnacles surrounding **the Table**. After passing broken ground on R, come to fallen wall, part of which appears from below as cairn. Path continues next to cliff edge on L; you can fork off **R**, directly uphill, to summit trig point on **Meall na Suiramach**.

❻ Follow broad path slightly downhill to cairn at cliff edge. Look straight down on to **the Table**, 100ft (30m) below. Turn **R** on wide path. After 1 mile (1.6km), path descends alongside cliff edge. As edge turns half-R, you should turn fully **R**. Path is faint, but reappears ahead contouring around steep grass slope. Above car park it turns straight downhill for final steep descent.

Raasay A Royal Refuge

7¾ miles (12.5km) 3hrs 45min **Ascent:** 820ft (250m) **2**
Paths: Small but clear paths, some tracks, 1 stile
Suggested map: OS Explorer 409 Raasay, Rona & Scalpay or 410 Skye – Portree & Bracadale
Grid reference: NG 555342 (on OS Explorer 410)
Parking: Ferry terminal at Sconser, Skye (or lay-by to east); Calmac ferries run each hour to Raasay

To Raasay's old iron mining railway.

❶ On Raasay, turn **L** on road. At **Inverarish**, turn **L** over bridge and divert **L** along shore. After playing field rejoin road, pass **Isle of Raasay Hotel** to junction.

❷ Continue ahead past neglected stable block, towards **Raasay House**, now outdoor centre. Just before it, turn **L** to **old pier**. Track continues below ramparts of old gun battery. Follow path around bay, until gate leads to shoreline path to **Eilean Aird nan Gobhar**. Check tides before crossing to tidal island.

❸ Head inland over rock knoll, then pass along L-H edge of plantation on muddy path overhung by rhododendron. Continue along shore of **North Bay**, with pine plantation on your R, round to headland. Go up briefly through low basalt cliff and return along its top. Head along **L** edge of plantation, to emerge through iron gate on to road.

❹ Turn **L** for 180yds (165m) to grey gate on **R**. Green track leads up and to **R** into craggy valley. At

walled paddock it turns **L** to join tarred road. Follow this down past lily lochan and turn **L** across dam. Join wide path running up under larch and rhododendron but, in 100yds (91m), bear **R** ('Temptation Hill Trail'). Side path on **R** leads to remains of Iron-Age broch (tower). Main path leads down to pass white church, then bends **R** and drops to tarred road.

❺ Turn sharp **L** up road for 200yds (183m), then **R** at white-topped waymark. Track shrinks to path as it bends **L** and climbs. It becomes forest track, passing more white waymarkers, finally reaching abandoned buildings of old iron **mine**.

❻ At tarred beyond, turn up **L** to signpost for Miners' Trail. Turn **R** on green track of former **railway**. Where **viaduct** has been removed, path scrambles down steeply and then climbs again to regain railbed. Blue-waymarked Miners' Trail turns off, but your route follows **railway** onwards, across stretch of moor and down to **ferry** terminal.

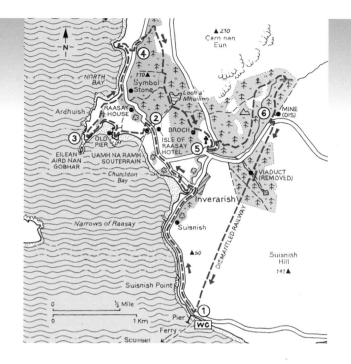

Portree Seeing Sea Eagles

2¾ miles (4.4km) 1hr 15min **Ascent:** 400ft (122m) **2**
Paths: Smooth, well-made paths, farm track, 3 stiles
Suggested map: OS Explorer 409 Raasay, Rona & Scalpay or 410 Skye – Portree & Bracadale
Grid reference: NG 485436 (on OS Explorer 410)
Parking: Daytime-only parking on main A855 above Portree Harbour. Small parking area at slipway

A lovely coastal walk to a raised beach called the Bile.

❶ Turn off **A855** on lane ('Budh Mor'), walk to shoreline then continue to small parking area. Tarred path continues along shore. After crossing footbridge, it passes under hazels. Path rounds headland to reach edge of level green field called **the Bile**.

❷ Wall runs up edge of **the Bile**. Ignore small gate, but turn **L** with wall on your R. Just before field corner pass large fuchsia bush. About 25yds (23m) later path forks. Turn **R**, crossing small stream and wall, to head along top edge of **the Bile**. Turn **R**, down fence, to field gate. Cross top of next field on old green path, to stile at its corner. See track just beyond.

❸ Turn sharp **L**, up track. At top it passes through 2 gates to reach stony road just to R of **Torvaig**. Turn **L** past house and cross foot of tarred road into gently descending track. It runs down between 2 large corrugated sheds and through gate with stile.

❹ Grassy path ahead leads down into **Portree**, but you can take short, rough, diversion to **Dun Torvaig** (ancient fortified hilltop) above. For **dun**, turn **L** along fence, and then **L** again on well-made path above. It leads to kissing gate above 2 sheds. Turn sharp **R** along fence for a few steps then bear **L** around base of small outcrop and head up on tiny path to **dun**. Remnants of dry-stone walling can be seen around summit. Return to gravel path, passing above Point **❹** to join wall on your **R**. Path leads down under goat willows into wood where it splits; stay close to wall and continue ahead.

❺ At 1st houses (The Parks Bungalow 5), keep downhill on tarred street. On L is entrance to **Cuillin Hills Hotel**. A few steps later, fork **R** on to stony path. At shore road, turn **R** across stream and at once turn **R** again on to path that runs up for 60yds (55m) to craggy little **waterfall**. Return to shore road and turn **R** to walk start.

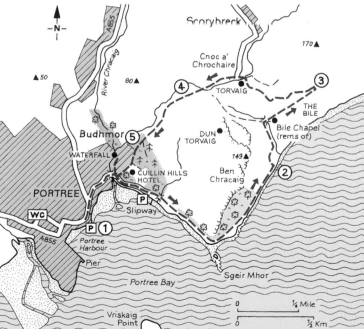

93 Ramasaig Waterstein Head

5¾ miles (9.2km) 3hrs 30min **Ascent:** 1,500ft (457m) ▲
Paths: Grassy clifftops and moorland, 1 stile
Suggested map: OS Explorer 407 Skye – Dunvegan
Grid reference: NG 163443
Parking: Ramasaig road end or pull-ins at pass ¾ mile (1.2km) north

Through crofting country and peat moors to a 1,000ft (305m) sea cliff.

❶ From end of tarmac, road continues as track between farm buildings, with bridge over **Ramasaig Burn**. After gate it reaches shed with tin roof. Bear **R** here and follow **L** bank of Ramasaig Burn to shore.

❷ Cross **burn** at ford and head up very steep meadow beside fence that protects cliff edge. There's awkward fence to cross half way up. At top, above **Ramasaig Cliff**, keep following fence on **L**. It cuts across to **R** to protect notch in cliff edge. From here (Point ❸), you could cut down to parking areas at road pass near by.

❸ Keep downhill alongside cliffside fence. At bottom, turf wall off to **R** provides another short-cut back to road. Clifftop walk now bears slightly **R** around V-notch of **Moonen Burn**. Small path crosses stream and continues uphill to rejoin clifftop fence, which soon turns slightly inland around another cliff notch.

Cliff-edge fence leads up and to **L**, to reach **Waterstein Head**. Here there is a **trig point**, 971ft (296m) above the sea – the 2nd highest sea cliff on Skye. Below you will see Neist Point lighthouse.

❹ Return for ¼ mile (400m) down to where fence bends to **R**, then continue ahead through shallow grassy col for slight rise to **Beinn Charnach**. Here bear **R** to follow gently rounded grass ridge line parallel with cliffs. Highest line along ridge is driest. Fence runs across, with grey gate at its highest point where it passes through col. Climb over gate and on up to cairn on **Beinn na Coinnich**.

❺ Continue along slightly rocky plateau for 300yds (274m) to southeast top. Now **Ramasaig** road is visible ¼ mile (400m) away on **L**. Go down to join quad bike track heading towards road. Just before reaching road, bike track crosses swampy col. This shows old and recent peat workings. Turn **R**, along road, passing above **Loch Eishort** to start.

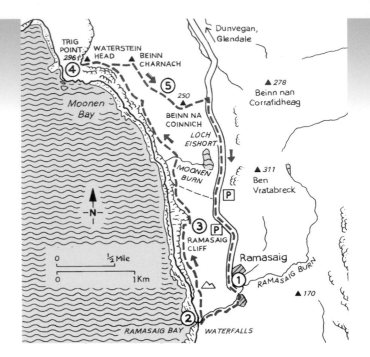

94 Strath Carron South Torridon Mountains

9 miles (14.5km) 5hrs **Ascent:** 1,700ft (518m) ▲
Paths: Well-made path, then track, no stiles. Note: During stalking season on Achnashellach Estate (15 September–20 October, not Sundays), keep strictly to route, which is right of way.
Suggested map: OS Explorer 429 Glen Carron & West Monar
Grid reference: NH 005484 **Parking:** On A890 below Achnashellach Station

Deer stalkers' paths lead into the mountains.

❶ Track to **station** runs up behind red phone box, then turns **R** to platform end. Cross line through 2 gates and head up stony track opposite, past waymarker arrow. After 100yds (91m) reach junction under power lines. Turn **L** on smooth gravel road to gate through deer fence. After ¼ mile (400m), look for cairn where new path turns back to **L**.

❷ Path goes back through deer fence at kissing gate, then runs up alongside **River Lair**. As slope steepens above tree-line, short side path on **L** gives view of **waterfall**. Well-maintained stalkers' path runs over slabs of bare sandstone. Cairn marks point where it arrives in upper valley, Coire Lair, with view to high pass at its head, 2 miles (3.2km) away.

❸ About 200yds (183m) after this 1st cairn, another marks junction of paths. Bear **R**, between 2 pools. Shortly there is 2nd junction with cairn. Bear **R**, on path that leaves corrie through wide, shallow col

350yds (320m) above. Conical cairn marks highest point. Path descends among drumlins and sandstone boulders, slanting down to **R** to join wooded **Allt nan Dearcag**. Path now runs down alongside this stream. Scattered forest damaged by fire and grazing side is on opposite side as path drops to footbridge. Bridge crosses side stream, **Allt Coire Beinne Leithe**, with **Easan Geal**, White Waterfalls, just above.

❹ At locked estate **hut**, track continues downhill, with gorge of **Easan Dorcha** (Dark Waterfalls) on **R**. After 1 mile (1.6km) turn **R** over stone bridge on **R** to track that runs up valley to **Coulin Pass** at its head.

❺ After pass, track goes through gate into plantations, then bends **R** to slant down side of Strath Carron. At Scottish Rights of Way Society signpost, follow main track ahead towards **Achnashellach**. Enter clear-felled area then cross bridge to reach mobile phone mast. Fork **L**, passing 2nd mast, and descend to reach junction above **station**.

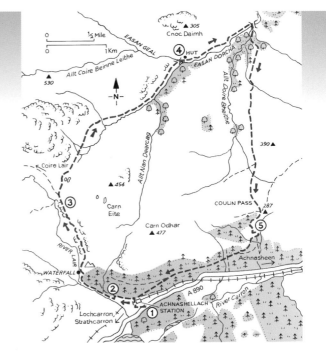

Loch Torridon The Diabaig Coast Path

9½ miles (15.3km) 6hrs Ascent: 1,805ft (550m) 🄐

Paths: Narrow, rough and wet in places, no stiles

Suggested map: OS Explorer 433 Torridon – Beinn Eighe & Liathach

Grid reference: NG 840575

Parking: Informal camp and caravan site above Inveralligin

In the footsteps of the fairy folk.

❶ Follow road **R**, past village green, over Abhainn Alligin, along shoreline for 100yds (91m), then up **R** among sandstone outcrops. Bear **L** under power line to join corner of tarmac driveway. Keep ahead to **Alligin Shuas**.

❷ Turn up road and then **L**, on road for Diabaig. As road steepens, you can take path ahead, rejoining road as it crosses high pass and runs down past linked **Loch Diabaigas Airde** and **Loch a'Mhullaich**.

❸ Turn off **L**, cross footbridge. Clear path leads out along high wall of valley, then zig-zags down spur, to grey gate. Descend through woods to white house, No 1 Diabaig. Turn **R** to old stone **pier**.

❹ Return up path you just came down to pass stone shed. Sign indicates turn to **R**, under outcrop and between boulders. Path heads up to small rock step with arrow mark, up to gate in fence and zig-zags into open gully, large crag on R. At top of this, it turns **R**

along shelf, with more crag above. Path slants gently down along foot of another crag, then up to col.

❺ From here path is small but clear. It bends **R** to **Loch a' Bhealaich Mhoir** then **L** below it to small **loch**. Follow stream down towards cottage, **Port Lair**.

❻ Pass above house, then slant gradually up away from sea. Path crosses head of bracken valley with ruined croft house into knolly area. Cross 2 branches of stream and ascend to cairn which marks where path bears **L** up spur. It now contours across meadow among knolls, at end of which it climbs pink rocks over final spur, with view up Loch Torridon to Liathach.

❼ Path descends slightly to cross high, steep slope of heather. Near end of slope, path forks. Take upper branch, through wide col. Boggy path descends towards **Alligin Shuas**. From gate above village, faint path runs down in direction of distant green shed. It descends through wood, then contours just above village to road above Point ❷. Retrace steps to start.

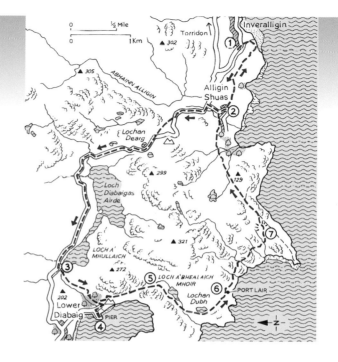

Gairloch Flowerdale Falls

5¼ miles (8.4km) 2hrs 45min Ascent: 800ft (244m) 🄐

Paths: Tracks and smooth paths, mostly waymarked, no stiles

Suggested map: OS Explorer 433 Torridon – Beinn Eighe & Liathach or 434 Gairloch & Loch Ewe

Grid reference: NG 807756 on OS Explorer 433

Parking: Beach car park, southern end of Gairloch

Porpoise-watching along the Gairloch shore.

❶ Cross road and head up to **R** of cemetery. Turn **L** at corner, into trees to track above. Turn **R** until footbridge leads on to wide path that descends. With wall corner ahead, turn **R** ('Flowerdale Waterfall'). Track descends to tarred driveway.

❷ Turn **L** to pass **Flowerdale House**. Way is marked with red-topped poles. Track passes to **L** of old barn and turns **R** at sign for **waterfall** to pass **Flowerdale Mains**. In ¼ mile (400m) pass concrete bridge on R.

❸ Follow main path, still to **L** of stream to footbridge, just before you get to **Flowerdale Waterfall**.

❹ Path leads up past **waterfall** to cross footbridge above. It runs up into pine clump, then turns back down valley. After another footbridge it joins rough track, to meet forest road beside Point ❸. Turn **L**, away from concrete bridge, through felled forest.

❺ Look for blue-topped pole marking path on **R** with

footbridge. It leads through meadowland and bracken with blue waymarker poles. Path bends **R** at old fence cornerpost and descends through bracken and birch to pass above and to **L** of enclosed field. Turn **R** under 2 large oak trees and cross stream to earth track.

❻ Turn **L** for few steps, until small bracken path runs up to **R** past waymarked power pole. Path bends **L** under oaks, then drops to rejoin earth track. This soon meets larger track, old road from Loch Maree to Gairloch. Turn **R** along this, through couple of gates, to **Old Inn** at **Charlestown**.

❼ Cross old bridge, and main road, to pier. Turn **R** at sign for Gairloch Chandlery, to tarmac path ('beach'). This passes to **L** of pinewood, then turns **R** into trees. It bends **L** and emerges to run along spine of small headland. Just before being carried out to sea it turns sharp **R**, and crosses above rocky bay to fort (An Dun). Duckboard path runs along back of beach, then turns **R** to car park.

Poolewe Great Wilderness

6½ miles (10.4km) 2hrs 45min **Ascent:** 250ft (76m) ⚠
Paths: Mostly good, but one short rough, wet section, 3 stiles
Suggested map: OS Explorer 434 Gairloch & Loch Ewe
Grid reference: NG 857808
Parking: In Poolewe, just up B8057 side street

Highland • Scotland

A pleasant walk around Loch Kernsary.

❶ Kissing gate beside public toilets leads to path that crosses Marie Curie Field of Hope to main road. Turn **L** to cross bridge over **River Ewe** then continue through village. At 40mph derestriction sign, there's white cottage on R. Beside it, tarred trackway has Scottish Rights of Way Society signpost for **Kernsary**.

❷ Follow track over cattle grid to new track that forks **L**. After 50yds (46m), keep ahead on path with wall on **L**. It passes through kissing gate into Cnoc na Lise, Garden Hill. This has been replanted as community wood with oak and birch trees. Another kissing gate leads out of young wood. Reconstructed path runs over bare sandstone slabs and under low-voltage power line. It crosses low spur to fine view of **Loch Kernsary** and remote, steep-sided hills of Great Wilderness, then goes over stream to **loch** side.

❸ Path follows L-H shore of **loch**, passing through patches of birch scrub. About half-way along **loch**, it suddenly deteriorates, becoming braided trod of boulder and bog. From stile at **loch** head, slant to **L** down meadow to footbridge under oak tree. Head up, with fence on R, to join track beside **Kernsary** farm.

❹ Turn **R**, through gate. Follow track past farm, to culvert crossing of **Kernsary River**. This becomes ford only after heavy rain. If needed, you will find footbridge 70yds (64m) upstream. After crossing, turn **R** on smooth track. New track bears **L**, away from **Loch Kernsary** towards hollow containing **Loch Maree**. After bridge over Inveran River is gate with ladder stile. Signs welcoming responsible walkers (and cyclists) reflect principles of Letterewe Accord. Soon come views of **Loch Maree**. The driveway of **Inveran** house joins from **L** and track starts being tarred.

❺ At sign, 'Blind Corners', green track on **L** leads down to point where narrow **loch** becomes wide river. Return to main track and follow it above then beside **River Ewe**. It reaches **Poolewe** just beside bridge.

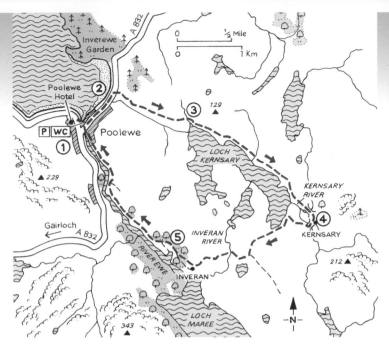

Loch Ness Monsters and Beasties

4¼ miles (6.8km) 2hrs 15min **Ascent:** 700ft (213m) ▲
Paths: Waymarked paths and tracks, no stiles
Suggested map: OS Explorer 416 Inverness, Loch Ness & Culloden
Grid reference: NH 522237 **Parking:** Forest Enterprise car park

Highland • Scotland

Overlooking Loch Ness and past the home of the Beast of Boleskine.

❶ From car park follow yellow waymarkers uphill near stream. After 100yds (91m), take path on **R** ('Loch View'). After bench, path contours briefly then turns up **L**, to higher viewpoint, then turns back sharply **R** and descends on earth steps through little crag to forest road. Turn **R** for 200yds (183m).

❷ Turn up **L** on footpath with more yellow waymarkers. Path has low, mossed wall alongside as it bends up to higher forest road. Turn **R** and walk for 150yds (137m) to sharp L-H bend. Keep ahead on small footpath through area of cleared forestry, then go steeply up to **L** under trees. At top, bear **L** along little ridge, dropping gently downhill to viewpoint.

❸ Return for 100yds (91m); bear **L** down other side of ridge. Path descends steeply to forest road. Sign indicates **Lochan Torr** an Tuill (picnic table near by).

❹ Return down forest road, past where you joined it. It climbs gently, then descends to sharp **R** bend where

you turned off earlier ('to Car Park') on side now facing you. After 150yds (137m), at another 'to Car Park' waymarker, turn **L** down path with low mossed wall to forest road below (Point ❷). Turn **L**, past red/green waymarker. Track kinks **L** past **quarry**.

❺ Where main track bends **R**, downhill, keep ahead on green track with red/green waymarker to emerge from trees at signpost. Follow this down to **R** towards **Easter Boleskine** house. Green waymarkers indicate diversion to **L** of house, to join its driveway track below. Follow this down to **B852**.

❻ Turn **R** for 50yds (46m). Below **L** edge of road is tarred track. Turn down past blue/green waymarker to cross this track, with two blue waymarkers leading into path beyond. Pass down to **R** of electricity transformers. At foot of slope, main path bears **R** with blue waymarker. It runs above **loch** shore and joins gravel track just below **Lower Birchwood House**. Tarred lane ahead leads up to **B852**, with car park just above on **R**.

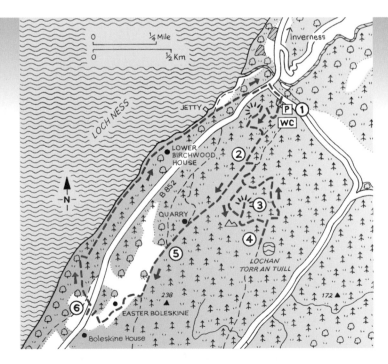

Strathpeffer The Falls of Rogie

10 miles (16.1km) 5hrs Ascent: 1,200ft (365m)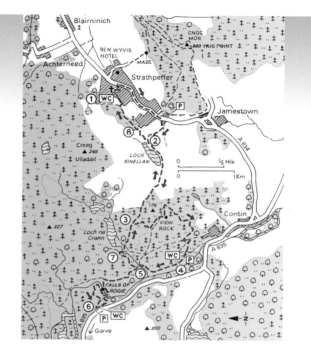
Paths: Waymarked paths and track, no stiles
Suggested map: OS Explorer 437 Ben Wyvis & Strathpeffer
Grid reference: NH 483582 **Parking:** Main square, Strathpeffer

From a spa to a salmon-leaping waterfall.

❶ Head along main road towards **Contin**. At edge of town, turn **R** at signpost for Garve then, at bend in lane, turn **L**, following another signpost.

❷ Pass round to **L** of **Loch Kinellan**, then keep ahead up faint path through gorse to corner of plantation. Join larger track leading into forest. After ¼ mile (400m) reach signpost.

❸ Turn **L** for **View Rock** on good path with green waymarkers. At **View Rock**, side-path diverts to **R** for viewpoint. After steep descent, ignore green path turning off to L and follow green waymarkers downhill. At forest road turn **L**, then back **R** for 60yds (55m) to path on **L**. Cross another forest road to car park

❹ At end of car park pick up wide path ('River Walk'). After stream culvert, main path bends up to **R**, past waymark to forest road. Turn **L** ('Garve'), and in 80yds (73m) bear **L**, heading slightly downhill.

❺ Go on for 600yds (549m), to small track on **L** ('**Falls of Rogie**'). At its foot, cross footbridge below

falls; turn **R**, upstream. Path has green waymarkers and after ¼ mile (400m) bends **L** away from river. Cross rocky ground to junction. Turn up **R**, to car park.

❻ Leave car park through wooden arch and follow green waymarkers back to bridge. Retrace outward route to Point ❺ and turn sharp **L** up forest road. leading uphill to 4-way junction.

❼ Turn **R** on smaller track to pass between boulders, then **L** on rutted path to rejoin same track higher up. After 600yds (549m) reach signpost at Point ❸. Keep ahead and retrace outward route to Point ❷. Turn **L** on tarred lane, which becomes track. Keep ahead towards house, but before it, turn **L** through kissing gate, with 2nd one beyond leading into plantation ('**Strathpeffer**').

❽ Follow main track straight ahead until you see **Strathpeffer** down on right. At next junction bear **R** down wood edge and turn **R** into town. Street on **L** leads past church with square steeple, where you turn down **R** to main square.

Mainland Orkney The Gloup Loop

4 miles (6.4km) 2hrs 30min Ascent: 93ft (28m)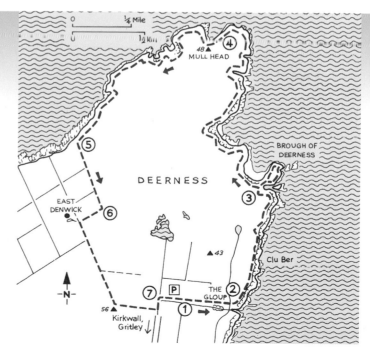
Paths: Continuous, 4 kissing gates, 2 stiles
Suggested map: OS Explorer 461 Orkney – East Mainland
Grid reference: HY 590079
Parking: Mull Head car park (free)
Note: Dogs are not allowed on this walk due to wildlife

An easy walk with an abundance of wildlife.

❶ Leave car park at R-H corner and follow direction sign along gravel path to **The Gloup**, where you will find 2 viewing platforms and information plaque. The word 'Gloup' comes from the old Norse word 'gluppa' meaning chasm and at 100ft (30m) deep it is a remarkable feat, formed by the force of the North Sea.

❷ Past **The Gloup** you will see red-painted kissing gate and directional sign pointing **L**. This will lead you along grassy footpath to **Brough of Deerness** (pronounced 'broch'), but a more interesting route, perhaps, is straight ahead and then **L** along cliff edge, also following grassy path.

❸ At **Brough** is another information plaque and, in cliff edge, precipitous stone staircase which takes you down cliff (take care here) and, by turning **R** at beach, into sheltered stony bay, Little Burra Geo. You will see, in edge of **Brough** wall, steep dirt path, which you can

climb with help of chain set into rock. This will take you to top of **Brough** so that you can explore ancient site here.

❹ Having climbed back to main route, another red-painted kissing gate on your **R** shows footpath leading along to cairn at **Mull Head**. From cairn path turns **L** and becomes much narrower, although still clear, taking you along northern cliff edge.

❺ Path turns sharp **L** just before wire fence and climbs uphill through moorland to another red-painted kissing gate.

❻ Turn **R** here and go down to yet another gate you can see in fencing above derelict farmhouse, **East Denwick**. Here turn **L** along wide track and climb hill until track becomes very overgrown and **L** turn travels downhill to small red-painted gate on your **L**.

❼ Narrow grass path through gate and between wire fences turns **R** and leads back into car park.

Walking in Safety

All these walks are suitable for any reasonably fit person, but less experienced walkers should try the easier walks first. Route finding is usually straightforward, but you will find that an Ordnance Survey map is a useful addition to the route maps and descriptions.

Risks

Although each walk has been researched with a view to minimising the risks to the walkers who follow its route, no walk in the countryside can be considered to be completely free from risk. Walking in the outdoors will always require a degree of common sense and judgement to ensure that it is as safe as possible.

- Be particularly careful on cliff paths and in upland terrain, where the consequences of a slip can be very serious.

- Remember to check tidal conditions before walking along the seashore.

- Some sections of route are by, or cross roads. Take care and remember traffic is a danger even on minor country lanes.

- Be careful around farmyard machinery and livestock, especially if you have children or a dog with you.

- Be aware of the consequences of changes of weather and check the forecast before you set off. Carry spare clothing and a torch if you are walking in the winter months. Remember that the weather can change very quickly at any time of the year, and in moorland and heathland areas, mist and fog can make route finding much harder. Don't set out in these conditions unless you are confident of your navigation skills in poor visibility. In summer remember to take account of the heat and sun; wear a hat and carry spare water.

- On walks away from centres of population you should carry a whistle and survival bag. If you do have an accident requiring the emergency services, make a note of your position as accurately as possible and dial 999.

Equipment

- The most important single item of equipment for country walking is a good pair of sturdy boots or walking shoes. Boots give better support to your ankles, especially in rough or hill country, and your feet need to be kept warm and dry in all conditions.

- Britain's climate is unpredictable, so warm and waterproof clothing is the next essential, but you don't need to spend a fortune on an Everest-specification jacket for a gentle stroll. There are many efficient and breathable alternatives which need not cost the earth. Waterproof trousers or gaiters are also a good idea and, as up to 40 per cent of body heat is lost through the head, a warm hat is essential.

- None of the walks in this book will take more than a day, but you will need a rucksack to hold extra clothing, food and drink for the longer walks. Look for one with about a 20 to 35-litre capacity, with stormproof pockets for your map, compass (a good ideal on any hill walk), camera and other bits and pieces.